FROM TRYOUTS TO CHAMPIONSHIPS

SHIPS FROM TRYOUTS TO CHAMPIONSH

FROM TRYOUTS TO CHAMPIONSHIPS

TRYOUTS TO CHAMPIONSHIPS FROM T

FROM TRYOUTS TO CHAMPIONSHIPS

SHIPS FROM TRYOUTS TO CHAMPIONSH

FROM TRYOUTS TO CHAMPIONSHIPS

TRYOUTS TO CHAMPIONSHIPS FROM T

FROM TRYOUTS TO CHAMPIONSHIPS

SHIPS FROM TRYOUTS TO CHAMPIONSH

FROM TRYOUTS TO CHAMPIONSHIPS

CHEERLEADING

FROM TRYOUTS TO CHAMPIONSHIPS

From the Editors and Writers of *Inside Cheerleading* Magazine

UNIVERSE

This edition first published in 2007
by UNIVERSE PUBLISHING
A division of Rizzoli International Publications, Inc.
300 Park Avenue South
New York NY 10010
www.rizzoliusa.com

Copyright © 2007, *Inside Cheerleading* Magazine
Design by Courtney Wilkes, *Inside Cheerleading* Magazine

2007 2008 2009 2010 / 10 9 8 7 6 5 4 3 2 1
First Edition

Printed in China

ISBN-13: 978-0-7893-15656
Library of Congress Control Number: 2007901406

CHEERLEADING

FROM TRYOUTS TO CHAMPIONSHIPS

Edited by Caitlin Leffel

Inside Cheerleading Magazine
Text by Theresa Crouse, Christie Griffin, Tara Jeroloman, Blanche Kapustin,
Chris Korotky, Sara McDaniel, Liza Mooney and Shane Womack

CHEERLEADING
FROM TRYOUTS TO CHAMPIONSHIPS

TABLE OF CONTENTS

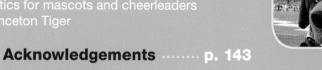

INTRODUCTION

"Where did cheerleading come from?"

That's a question we hear time and time again as we travel to camps, competitions, seminars, coaches' conferences, and countless other events throughout the year. We also hear, "I'm a high school cheerleader but want to transition to All Star. How can I make that happen?" And, "How do I increase my flexibility so that my stunts look better?" And even, "How can my team make it to the Cheerleading Worlds?" These questions reflect the many directions that cheerleading offers young athletes today and also show some of the key attributes that cheerleaders are known for: the desire to improve, the energy to do more, spirit, and respect for their fellow cheerleaders and those who came before them.

Cheerleading has come a long way since its beginnings at a Minnesota football game in the 1880s. Today, cheerleading is one of the nation's most popular sports and is gaining recognition around the world. It's a challenging physical activity whose participants train year-round at different levels on teams and at camps, and it's a competitive sport with an annual World Championship covered by ESPN. To help cheerleaders across the globe continue to soar to new heights, we set out to produce a magazine that is chock-full of the information that today's cheerleaders need to know, presented in a cool and entertaining manner. With the popularity of the magazine, we thought the next step would be to develop a book that could serve as a guide for veterans, an introduction for newcomers, a resource for coaches, and a fun, informative read for all.

The writers, contributors, and editors at *Inside Cheerleading* have strong backgrounds as cheerleaders, gymnasts, and mascots. They're people who have succeeded on their personal journeys and who now want to share their passion for the sport with others. From executing the perfect pep rally that spurs a team to victory, to winning National Championships and competing at the Cheerleading Worlds, our team has done it all. With this book, our knowledge and expertise is literally at your fingertips.

As cheerleading has grown up, its offspring—high school, All Star, college, and professional—have gone in different directions to achieve great things. With the magazine and now this book, we've aimed to give you, cheerleaders in each of these areas, targeted information. But no matter what type of spirit leading you're involved in, you're still first and foremost cheerleaders, and you're unified by some of the core techniques and values that have been with cheerleading since its beginnings. With that in mind, we start the book with a look back at the roots of the sport and its amazing growth in modern times. Then we cover everything from tryouts to fashion to life as a mascot to the future of the sport.

In the first chapter Lawrence "Herkie" Herkimer, widely credited as the father of modern cheerleading, shares his personal experiences. As he spoke to us and reminisced about how far the sport he loves and has dedicated so much of his life to has come, small tears welled up in his eyes and his voice shook. It was inspiring for us to hear firsthand what cheerleading has meant to him. Strength, discipline, commitment, and focus are values he learned through cheerleading—the same values that those who have followed him in the sport promote today. He built a base of knowledge and shared it with others, motivating cheerleaders at every level, of every type, to do their best. And now, just as Herkie did so many years ago, we hope this book will inspire you to be the best you can be, in cheerleading and beyond.

Chris Korotky
Publisher, *Inside Cheerleading*

Liza Mooney
Editor, *Inside Cheerleading*

CHAPTER 1

Y ou explode with spirit, fly high in your partner stunts and baskets, and make sure you hit each choreographed move. But do you ever wonder about the stories behind the pyramids, the pep rallies, and the competitions? Like how the Herkie jump got its name? Or why the "spirit stick" became the coveted award at summer camp?

"Father of modern cheerleading" Lawrence Herkimer (center of pyramid) has been supporting cheerleaders since the sport's earliest days.

Cheerleading

Then...and Now!

Herkimer started stunting early. Here, he's flying high and incorporating acrobatics into traditional crowd-leading techniques.

▶▶ **Warning!**

This is not your grandmother's cheerleading book! Back in her day, cheerleaders were clad in bulky sweaters and carried oversize props; contemporary squads sport peppy skirts, diminutive poms, and a whole lot of athletic prowess. But today's complicated stunt sequences and intricate routines do have their roots in the early days. Like the sport's signature stunt—the pyramid—these advanced, specialized moves grew out of the single jumps and simple chants invented by spirited students long ago.

In barely more than a hundred years, cheerleading has evolved from a few men at a handful of American schools hollering at football games to nearly four million coed acrobats yelling, stunting, and dancing for crowds, not to mention competing against teams from around the world.

But let's not get ahead of ourselves—cheerleading's pioneers deserve a nod. Their will and determination—not to mention their lung capacity—have helped as much as any stunt or move to make cheerleading what it is today. We'll start at the beginning.

100+ Years of Cheerleading

1880s
First Yell Recorded
(Princeton University)

1890s
First Organized Cheerleading
(University of Minnesota)

1919
First Recorded Pep Rally Fundraiser
(University of Kansas)

1920s
First Female Yell Leaders
First Gymnastics in Cheerleading
(University of Minnesota)
First Flash-Card Cheering
(Oregon State University)

1930s
First Pompon Routines Performed

1949
First Cheer Camp
(Sam Houston State University)

1950s
First Spirit Booster Ribbons

1954
First Spirit Stick

1960s
NFL Organizes Professional
Cheerleading Teams

1970s
Training for Coaches First Offered
at Cheer Camps

1972
Dallas Cowboy Cheerleaders First
Performed

1980s
First Coaches' Conference
First AACCA Safety Courses

2004
First USASF World Championships
of All Star Cheerleading

From simple stunts...

to intricate pyramids...

to World Championships!

▶ Give Me a "Y"!

"Ray, Ray, Ray! TIGER, TIGER, SIS, SIS, SIS! BOOM, BOOM, BOOM! Aaaaah! PRINCETON, PRINCETON, PRINCETON!" This nonsensical sentence composed of short, choppy words was a Princeton student's imitation of the train that took the university's athletes and spectators to away football games. Little did he know then, in the 1880s, that he'd invented the first cheer in the United States! Over a century later Princeton students and alumni still cheer their teams on with "the locomotive."

▶ From the Yell to the Cheer

In 1884 a Princeton graduate named Thomas Peebles accepted a teaching job at the University of Minnesota. He took "the locomotive" with him and shared it with his students. In November 1898 Johnny Campbell and five other University of Minnesota undergraduates were chosen to lead the students' yelling section at the last game of the season, making Campbell and his squad the world's first official cheerleaders. After the game the student newspaper printed the fans' most popular cheer: **"Rah, Rah, Rah! Sku-u-mar, Hoo-Rah! Hoo-Rah! Varsity! Varsity! Varsity, Minn-e-So-Tah!"**

▶ Building Spirit, Garnering Influence

In the fall of 1919 a cheer "stunt" proved this new "Sport of Spirit" could not only command the attention of the student body, but also incite them to act! In those days a school's athletic reputation was judged by the size of its football stadium, rather than by the quality of its team. The University of Kansas Jayhawks were ignored by football programs at larger schools because their two-thousand-seat McCook Stadium was considered puny and attendance at games was low. But when the school's football team nearly defeated the powerhouse University of Nebraska Cornhuskers, a University of Kansas student named Shirley Windsor took matters into his own hands.

He convinced the school to stop classes the next day and to hold a gigantic gathering he called a "pep rally." At the rally, Windsor and two fellow yell leaders pleaded the case for building a bigger stadium, leading the four thousand students present with passionate cheers and lots of noise. Within an hour, each student there had committed to donating sixty dollars, enough to build a gigantic thirty-thousand-seat stadium! This event kicked off the tradition of spirit-based fund-raising that cheerleading is known for today.

▶ The *Roaring* '20s

World War I brought changes to cheerleading. When men went to fight, women replaced them in the workforce, in the more traditionally male roles at home, and even as yell leaders. Like their male counterparts, the female cheerleaders stood front and center, leading students in cheers to encourage their football teams. When the war ended, the men returned, and coed squads were formed all over the country.

Meanwhile, fancy moves were starting to mingle with the cheers. In the 1920s, the University of Minnesota cheerleaders were the first to use gymnastics and tumbling to get the crowd's attention. On the West Coast, Lindley Bothwell, a cheerleader at Oregon State University, created the first flash-card cheering section.

The Father of Modern Cheerleading

Two decades later a Dallas teenager named Lawrence "Herkie" Herkimer (see "My Story" on page 19) entered the picture. As a young man, Herkimer suffered from a stutter, which he controlled by mastering balancing feats such as walking along a railroad track. His acrobatic skills led him to his school's cheerleading squad, and there, he discovered he never stuttered when he spoke in rhymes.

Having conquered his speech impediment through cheerleading in high school, Herkimer went on to cheer in college at Southern Methodist University (SMU), alongside television producer Aaron Spelling! After graduation he returned to Dallas, and in order to provide a unifying body for the growing sport he loved, formed the National Cheerleading Association (NCA). The NCA held a camp every summer where, with the help of an English teacher, cheerleaders could write cheers which Herkimer would then set to acrobatic movements. The fifty-two girls who attended the inaugural NCA camp were wowed by Herkie's gymnastics and excitedly took what they learned back to their own schools.

Top: Herkie shows off his moves at one of NCA's first camps.
Bottom: NCA camp's earliest staff.

Herkie's camps grew in popularity with each passing year. During camp, cheerleaders would meet squads from other schools, work together, and learn from each other; and at the end of the week, ribbons would be awarded to the most talented teams in several categories.

▶▶ Spirit in a Stick

In the 1950s NCA camp instructors began awarding trophies in a ceremony held at the end of the camp week. While the trophies were intended to reward the most talented squads, the instructors also wanted to recognize the most spirited ones. As the story goes, an instructor pulled a branch off a tree and tied award ribbons around it. When the campers thought all of the trophies had been passed out, the instructor pulled out this surprise award for spirit, presented it, and the campers cheered wildly. From that point on, the "spirit stick" became the most important award a team could receive at the end of camp.

▶ Along Came the Poms & Boosters

Not long after Lawrence Herkimer formed his cheerleading camps, he had a revelation about the future. When he got his first glimpse of a color TV at the 1964-65 World's Fair, he realized that the small metal batons his cheerleaders were using would be nearly invisible on a television screen. So he had the cheerleaders incorporate pompons into their routines. He made his by tying bright crepe paper to little sticks, which made the props easier to see on the big screen.

Pompons, uniforms, and other types of cheer gear soon became mainstays, presenting the new sport with a new dilemma: who would pay for what? Herkie came up with the idea of selling spirit boosters to help cheerleaders buy their outfits and props. School colors, logos, and yells were printed on ribbons, buttons, pennants, megaphones, and even small, plastic footballs. It was a win-win solution: students sported their purchases at games and cheerleaders had a way to pay for their cheerleading uniforms and equipment.

As schools have become savvier about fund-raising, many have organized separate booster clubs to help support their sports organizations. But it's not uncommon for cheerleading squads to work with these clubs to sell booster ribbons and other kinds of spirit wear. Nowadays, some schools even have online spirit shops!

A Modern Revolution

The biggest change in cheerleading from Herkie's early days is its evolution into a highly athletic activity—an evolution actually inspired by an athlete from another sport. Herkimer credits gymnastics superstar Nadia Comaneci with changing the landscape for girls in cheerleading. Girls became interested in gymnastics (which fed into cheerleading) when they watched the attractive, petite Comaneci excel in the 1976 Olympic Games in Montreal. Prior to this time, boys generally did the gymnastics and girls danced.

With this increased athleticism came the natural desire to showcase talent. In the 1980s and 1990s high school and college cheer programs gained competitive outlets for demonstrating their skills. The Universal Cheerleaders Association (UCA) held its first High School Cheerleading National Championships in 1980 and the exposure—these championships are now broadcast on ESPN—spawned tremendous growth and development in cheerleading. The NCA held its first High School National Championships in 1981. Ultimately, the NCA has established December as its Nationals month, following the end of the high school football season.

The movement of cheerleaders from the sidelines onto the field marked a dramatic shift in how cheerleading has been portrayed and perceived. Supporters of this shift praise the change from the stereotypical role of cheering while non-supporters, who view cheering as a support activity and not a sport unto itself, disagree. Either way, over the years, the popularity (and positive influence!) of programs in both competitive and support-based cheerleading is resounding proof that one need not take precedence over the other.

Over time sideline cheering has become more athletically challenging. Here Air Force Academy showcases talent and athleticism.

Above left: Professional cheerleading has come a long way from only dancing and shaking poms. Some professional sports teams now have co-ed cheerleading teams to incorporate stunts and pyramids such as this cupie.

Above right and below: These days college squads split their time between the sidelines and the competition mat but are careful to follow industry guidelines and safety regulations no matter where they are.

Cheerleaders at the NBA All Star game **(above)** take a minute out of their performance on the court to pose for a picture.

The Influence of NFL Cheerleading

By the 1960s cheerleaders were the norm at college and high school football games and various other college sports. Then the NFL came along and shook things up! In the early '70s, when professional football teams started organizing their own cheer squads, they chose to leave the traditionally collegiate look of cheerleading at the campus. In 1976, when the Dallas Cowboys played in Super Bowl X, all eyes were on the cheerleaders, as they performed in front of seventy-five million television viewers. While many were impressed by the squad's complex dance moves, others found their revealing outfits scandalous and inappropriate.

Cheerleading has changed drastically since the first sighting of cheerleaders in professional sports leagues. Professional sports cheerleaders are not always the all-girl dancers that once were associated with this title. More and more teams in both the NBA and NFL are moving toward co-ed teams that resemble the cheerleaders on the sidelines and courts of college games. Now, sideline chants and cheers are heard from the stands for the crowd to yell along with, rather than simply watching the girls dancing along to the music.

In fact, three United States presidents, a Supreme Court justice, several senators and countless other accomplished individuals were once cheerleaders! The sport has helped countless people to develop the ability to speak comfortably in front of crowds, to work together with others, and to support their communities.

▷ Safety First

Any cheer coach will tell you that their main concern in the sport is safety. The NCA advocates perfection before progression, and the organization's level-based system requires that cheerleaders master the sport's basic moves before attempting the more difficult ones. When the NCA discovered that the double-back, a difficult tumbling pass, was often being taught prematurely, it banned the move from all NCA competitions.

In 2001 the United States All Star Federation (USASF) was formed as the governing body to regulate All Star cheerleading. The USASF echoed the NCA's attention to safety, and soon secured its own set of safety guidelines by initiating rules and standards for the industry to follow, and by credentialing athletes and coaches. The USASF goes as far as requiring coaches to pass written tests and to meet with certified instructors who teach how certain skills should be developed and moves performed.

▷ Cheering on the Up and Up

What a future cheerleading has in store! Along with the USASF, organizations such as SITA (Spirit Industry Trade Association) and OSIP (Organization of Spirit Industry Providers) have helped level the playing field and bring structure and continuity to what was once a sport moving in too many different directions. Now that the sport is better governed, it's become the real deal, with countries all over the world paying attention and taking steps to follow the United States' lead. In fact, nearly two dozen international teams competed against American teams in the 2006 USASF World Championships of All Star cheerleading.

Growing pains have helped the sport to develop, kinks of all kinds have been worked out, and the activity of cheerleading is flying as high as its tallest pyramid. Take a minute and imagine what the activity will be like just ten or fifteen years from now. Olympic proportions, perhaps!

As stunting has become more advanced, industry guidelines have developed as well and now advocate using additional spots.

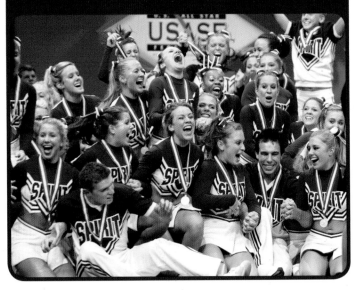

Following USASF guidelines paid off for Spirit of Texas, which celebrated a win at the 2005 USASF World Championships.

"How I Became the Father of Modern Cheerleading"

I actually didn't mean to build an empire. I was so enthused about being a cheerleader for four years in high school that I wanted to give that experience to other kids as well.

I was too small to play football or basketball, so I got into gymnastics. I went to SMU and was a cheerleader there, but then I was drafted and went off to the navy. After that I came back to SMU where I cheered for two more years. One summer I held a cheerleading clinic at SMU; then I started branching out. I hired instructors and staff and trained them. In those days the cheerleaders were the ambassadors of school spirit and sportsmanship. They weren't performing a lot of complicated stunts; they concentrated more on getting school spirit started among the student body, with pep rallies, and decorating the boys' lockers. Then in the 1980s, when the competitions started, cheerleaders started doing a lot more intricate things. It is amazing how much gymnastic and athletic ability the kids have now. It's a wonderful win-win situation. When kids get on a cheerleading squad and are out in front of an audience all the time, they learn to do a lot of things that help later on in the working world. If you've learned how to be a leader early on, that skill can mean the difference between being the head of a company and being a follower later.

Cheerleading has also been a great atmosphere in which to raise my three daughters. We spent every summer traveling around to camps, and my girls met so many wonderful kids. Cheerleaders

develop friendships easily. They have been great role models for my daughters—two of whom have gone on to become instructors themselves.

I had no idea that cheerleading would ever grow into the industry that it is today. When I borrowed six hundred dollars from my father-in-law to start my cheer camp, he thought I was crazy! I printed up my first circular about the camps and was able to pay him back at the end of the summer. He still thought I was nuts when I quit my job as an SMU professor and went into the cheer business full-time. But for the last ten years of his life, he worked for me! So in the end, it worked out fine for everybody.

Squad: Southern Methodist University (SMU)
Hometown: Aventura, Fla.
Interesting Fact: Herkimer received QSIP's first Lifetime Achievement Award in 2006.

CHAPTER 2

Cheerleading's future bodes well for those considering getting into the sport—there are now more options than ever. You can choose to go the traditional route and try out for a school squad; or, if you're in the market for something more competitive, you can join an All Star squad. Either way, you are assured an activity that's fun and challenging, and a new group of friends.

Regardless of the type of squad you choose, once you are a cheerleader, you can expect all eyes to be on you. Whether cheering on a team at game time or performing in a competition, when a cheerleader dons his or her uniform, he or she is an ambassador for the school or team and often the community as well. Keep this in mind as you make your way to the squad that's right for you.

Navy's college cheerleaders get great exposure, leading a crowd packed with peers, alumni, and the college's biggest fans.

Types of

Squads

Left: Admiration starts early! Auburn's cheerleaders make time to pose with even the littlest tigers.
Top right: Cheerleading's "peewees" gain valuable experience by competing at a young age.
Bottom right: Bright lights, loud music, and poms appeal to cheerleaders as young as four years old.

Great Beginnings

Even the youngest cheerleader wants to look and feel like the real thing, and "peewee" cheerleading programs can be a fun way for little ones to get a taste of the sport. The Pop Warner Little Scholars program offers cheerleading for kids as young as four years old. In the traditional program that runs from August through December, the squads cheer for the Pop Warner peewee football teams. There is also a competitive program that runs from January through July, where youngsters compete against teams of the same age-group.

Middle school–aged kids can also get a leg up on cheerleading by joining recreational squads. These programs are often designed to feed into high school programs. As their name suggests, these squads don't compete, but many of them use an All Star facility and its coaches to prepare for success at a higher level. While practice times vary, most require at least a weekly commitment during football or basketball season.

Toward the end of eighth grade, it's time to start thinking about high school cheerleading. Most high schools have freshman programs, and they often work with the middle schools that feed into them to coordinate cheer clinics and tryouts in the late spring. The clinics last one to two weeks and are held before squads are chosen. If you're moving to another region, or your middle school doesn't work with your area high school to set up tryout clinics, you might ask your new school about its tryout process. If possible, do so before mid-spring, to avoid missing tryouts! (See chapter 3 for more on tryouts.)

❯ **High School**

High school is the quintessential time to cheer. It's also when there's the greatest opportunity for cheerleaders at all levels of experience. So even if you have never cheered before, now's your chance! The most traditional and widely known kind of high school cheering is sideline cheering (also known as crowd leading). Its goal is to energize classmates and fans rooting for the school's team. Wherever there's a school with a sports team, there's a need for these kinds of cheerleaders.

Most high school cheer-leaders cheer for their school's sports teams, though some schools do have squads that compete. Some high schools have also created squads that are specialized and divided by focus. Pom squads, for instance, only cheer and dance, while other kinds of squads specialize in tumbling and stunts. High schools may also choose to divide squads according to the sport for which they cheer—such as football or basketball.

High school cheerleaders like those at Dunbar High must create sideline spirit even during football season's coldest nights.

The Cheer Cycle

Like any sport, there's a standard cycle to high school cheering. Spring tryouts start the process and camps continue it in the mid-summer. From then, depending upon the sport you're cheering for, you either keep cheering in the fall (for football, for example) or break, then start up again in the winter (for basketball or hockey, for example). Squads that cheer for soccer usually do so right up until tryout time again the following spring. There's little rest for the weary in this rowdy sport!

Spring: Tryouts

Winter: Basketball, Hockey

The Cheer Cycle

Summer: Camp

Fall: Football

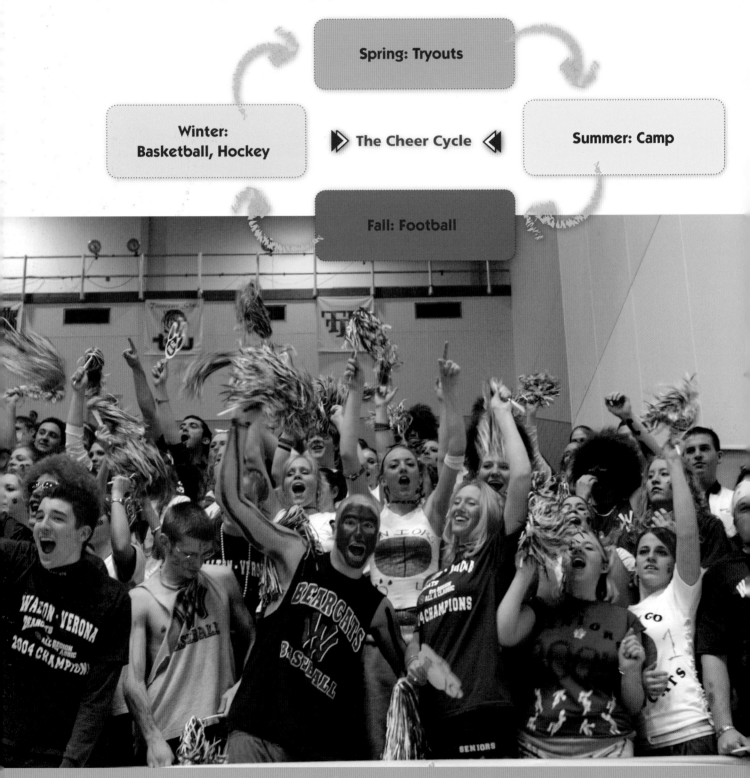

Rowdy fans respond with enthusiasm during a basketball pep rally.

Bearcat cheerleaders lead the crowd with cheers and chants all through the game.

Preps & Pep Rallies

A cheerleader's work starts well before game day. During the week leading up to a big game, cheerleaders work to pep up the players with some favorite "go get 'ems!" They may hand out goody bags filled with treats, or decorate coolers filled with sports drinks or flavored ice pops to pass out after practices. They may even go as far as decorating lockers with good-luck wishes.

A big game is not complete without a proper pep rally. A time-honored tradition, pep rallies generate excitement before the game and give the students a chance to salute the teams. School cheerleaders generally decide the format of the pep rally and work hard in advance to perfect routines. Most pep rallies are held in the school gymnasium during the school day, the week of the game. With the cheerleaders at the helm, rallies consist of cheers, chants, funny skits, class competitions, even pranks—all in good humor.

Pre-Game Show

The cheerleaders' "kickoff" in any regular-season game is the pre-game show. There's always a standing opportunity before a game to captivate and win over the crowd. Consider a basketball game: It's a great idea for cheerleaders, after warming up, to walk into the stands, where they can meet and greet the players' parents and say hello to friends. They can teach the fans some cheers and ask them to join in by yelling these chants during the game. If the band is ready to roll, the cheerleaders may dance the fight song and lead the crowd in chants during team warm-up. Depending on time, they can choose to perform a stunt or two to keep the crowd entertained.

Perhaps one of the most exhilarating "rushes" of cheering is when the players come onto the field or court. That's when the crowd goes wild! To heighten the excitement, cheerleaders may choose to put up what's called a run-through. This is typically a huge, decorated sign—anchored by two large metal poles on either end—that the players tear through as they make their grand entrance. Cheerleaders can put up shoulder stands to hold the poles. While they're performing this stunt, the remaining squad members can show spirit by doing simple tumbling passes, such as back handsprings and back tucks.

Opposite: Jackson Academy cheerleaders fire up the crowd.
Below: High school cheerleaders rush onto the field with their players.

Game On!

While the players are lining up on the field, the cheerleaders have the chance to stunt, jump, or chant, any of which signal the start of the game. From then on, all eyes should be on the game and all cheerleading actions should directly reflect what's happening on the court or the field. But that doesn't mean that it's break time! Cheerleaders need to be mini-experts on the sport for which they're cheering and learn the rules, calls, and regulations. If they don't, fans will likely notice, and the cheerleaders' credibility will be at stake.

Homecoming

Homecoming week and the weekend that follows—generally held during football or basketball season—is a showcase for spirit and is steeped in tradition. The biggest pep rallies of the year usually take place during homecoming week; and the homecoming game itself is the one alumni travel back for, students and local fans turn out for, and cheerleaders live for! Cheerleaders often work with the school faculty and student government to create a different theme for each day of this exciting week. "Backwards Day" and "School Spirit Day" are examples. It's also the most popular time of year to hold fund-raisers and encourage students to sport their booster ribbons.

All Star squads train many hours a week to syn-chronize and time routines for competitions like CHEERSPORT, the largest competition in the world with more than twenty-five thousand participants.

▷ All Star

All Star programs are off-campus cheerleading programs designed to provide a more competitive outlet for cheerleaders. Instead of supporting a school's sports team, their primary focus is preparing for competitions. Cheerleading gyms form the All Star teams which generally include members from several area high schools. Most All Star gyms place their cheerleaders on competition teams based on age and individual skill. Mirroring the school tryout period, gyms typically form their teams in late April to early May. Most gyms have all-girl and coed squads.

Like school teams, most All Star teams select a cheerleading camp to attend in mid-summer. The first round of competitions begins in October and practices leading up to them can be intense. Most teams practice three times each week for one-and-a-half to two hours at a time. This does not include the weekly tumbling instruction that generally lasts an hour. All Star is a year-round sport, and squads average six to ten competitions each year, so the eleven-month training season comes down to just a few minutes on display at a few key competitions.

All Star cheerleading is a sport, and like every sport, it has rules. The USASF over-sees the sport by making safety regulations and certifying both coaches and athletes. Level one is the most basic; level five the most advanced. At the end of each All Star season, coaches re-evaluate each team's skill level and determine, according to USASF guidelines, if it is ready to advance to the next level.

All Flipped Out: An Alternative for the Burnt-Out Gymnast

Until the advent of All Star squads, there wasn't much crossover between gymnasts and cheerleaders. But now, All Star cheerleading has become a natural progression for gymnasts who either have reached their full potential in gymnastics or want a change.

Gymnasts are used to competing and training, but the opportunities for them to do so at a collegiate level are slim and only the most talented can pursue the sport past high school. Competitive cheerleading offers a great alternative for gymnasts who are tired of the individual performance pressure, but still love to flip and jump. In All Star cheering, they can continue to execute and polish their tumbling passes—such as round-off back-handspring fulls and double fulls—plus, because of their gymnastics skills, they usually have an easy time picking up group stunting, choreography, and all the rest. With the increasing level of difficulty in tumbling and stunting, the number of gymnasts gravitating to cheerleading is expected to grow in the years ahead.

All Stars at their best, performing in some of the country's most elite competitions.
Left to right: America's Best, COA, JAMZ, The American Championships, Spirit Cheer, CHEERSPORT, AmeriCheer, Cheerleading World, UCA, JAMfest, and Cheer Ltd.'s CANAM

College cheerleaders work hard to raise spirits high. They balance heavy school schedules with demanding practices, games, and community events.

►► College

Cheering at the college level offers a great mix of school and All Star cheerleading. It's a form of sideline cheering that involves more activity than traditional school cheering with less of the competitive pressure of All Star cheering. At the collegiate level, there aren't separate squads for sideline cheering and competitions. The teams cheer at games as well as participate in at least one big competition each year, typically either an NCA- or UCA-sponsored one. Many schools select as many as forty-five cheerleaders each year; half are considered the junior varsity squad, and the other half the varsity squad.

Colleges dictate which sports their cheerleaders cheer for. Many cheer for multiple ones as well as participate in community events—such as alumni events, fund-raisers, recruitment programs, and award ceremonies. One cheerleader says his team was even hired to attend a wedding reception!

One skill that every college cheerleader needs is time management. College cheerleaders have heavy schedules, and unlike high school, parents are not present, watching over their kids' shoulders. College cheerleaders can count on three practices a week, each lasting three hours. That's in addition to game days, travel days, and special appearances, not to mention time spent studying (most schools require cheerleaders to maintain at least a 2.0 grade point average). Bottom line, there's little time left for boredom!

► Silent Spirit

Your college has no spirit group at all? Maybe there used to be a cheer squad but people lost interest in it over time. Maybe the athletic teams are not big enough to attract attention.

It doesn't matter. You know what you need to do. Take a look at your college—athletic programs, competition with rival schools, and community-college events—and determine how a spirit program would add to campus life. Schedule an appointment with the director of athletics or the dean of student activities to ask why the school does not have a spirit organization and listen to the response. There may be a strong reason for not organizing a cheer squad, but if there isn't, let that person know you'd like to start one. If he or she gives you the green light, go for it! Once you have official approval, see if your school is willing to help you with other things, such as activity funds and facility use.

Next, start recruiting. Post advertisements asking people interested in being part of the spirit squad to contact you so that you can gauge the level of interest. If enough people are interested, ask the school for space and a regular time slot for practices. Then post new advertisements letting everyone know about your initial meeting. If too many people show up, announce the dates a clinic will be held as well as a tryout date. Enlist help from the athletics staff. For judges, try to include one athletics staff member, a dance instructor, and one coach or player from the athletic teams for which you'll be cheering.

How many people do you need to start the program? The earliest spirit programs used four or more cheerleaders. With four, you have two bases, a flyer, and a back spotter for stunts. Four people with a passion can rouse a crowd just as well as forty!

UK: Lots to Cheer About

The University of Kentucky (UK) has long been considered the pre-eminent program in college cheerleading. The squad has finished in the top ten every year of the UCA National College Championships and holds more titles than any other Division 1-A program. The squad performs at every UK football and men's basketball game and attends numerous charity and community events. UK has two squads (similar to varsity and junior varsity); each includes eight to ten men and eight to ten women. The blue squad covers chief athletics, charity, and special events, while the white squad focuses on traditional and sideline cheering. Members of both squads are eligible for the competition team.

Since tryouts are held in the spring, incoming freshmen must attend the spring clinics, arrange a campus visit with the cheer coach, or submit a video tryout. There are three days of tryout clinics and judges make cuts throughout. Women are expected to perform a toss shoulder stand, a toss heel stretch, a stunt combination with only one transition, an original cheer, a back tuck, a backhandspring back tuck, and two other gymnastic skills. Those who make the blue squad generally far surpass what's required of them while those who make the white squad have shown the judges their future potential. All blue squad members receive a scholarship equal to the cost of in-state tuition.

Below: The University of Kentucky works hard to protect its reputation as a collegiate powerhouse cheer team.
Bottom left: The 2006 UK squad after taking home first place at UCA's College Nationals.

"Ushering in a New Generation of Cheer"

I was always an athlete growing up, and when I went to college at the University of Oklahoma, I saw cheerleading as a way to continue to participate in athletics. Some of my fraternity brothers were trying out for the cheerleading team, so I decided to give it a try as well. I think what I gained most from making and being on the team was an appreciation of the athleticism of the sport and how much a well-coordinated cheerleading effort can do to get a crowd involved at a game.

During my summer breaks while in college, I worked as an instructor for NCA. After graduation, I was considering going to law school when Lawrence Herkimer offered me a full-time position. I thought working for him would be a great way to save some money for law school, and initially, I didn't see this kind of a job as a long-term thing. But I quickly became general manager and my fondness for the activity continued to grow. I saw an opportunity to transform what cheerleading was, and so two years later (in 1975) I left to start my own company.

My goal was to make cheerleading more athletic, to add stunts and combinations not done at the time to the traditional crowd-leading routines. We began to develop different stunts as well as the techniques for building. Those techniques, such as climbing and bracing, are still used today. We demonstrated and taught these techniques at camps and showed cheerleaders how to integrate these new elements into their game-day routines. We were the first to put the elements of these routines and combinations to music; and after seeing our demonstrations, squads would go back and develop their own routines for games, and eventually, competitions.

With our Varsity Fashions division, we revolutionized the cheerleading uniform. We took the traditional sweater and box-pleated skirt combination and transformed it into a functional and stylish piece that reflects the athleticism of the sport. Though our styles continue to change with the times, the core philosophy of creating uniforms that embrace both fashion and function still rings true today.

In 1980 we introduced the UCA High School Cheerleading National Championships, cheerleading's first championship competition. The first year the competition was broadcast through TVS, the largest programmer of syndicated-sports content in the country at the time. The idea was that television was the best way to help the sport grow to new levels. We wanted our brand and our style on television for all to see. A few years into the competition, the broadcast moved to ESPN. Eventually we brought our UCA College Cheerleading National Championships to television, followed by the UCA All Star Cheerleading National Championships.

by Jeff Webb

While professional level is the pinnacle in other sports, this is not the case in cheerleading. To use a cheerleading term, college cheerleading is the top of the pyramid. Since professional cheerleading squads are dance teams, college is the most elite level of traditional cheerleading. The great college squads balance all of the talent, athleticism, and entertainment value of a competitive sport with traditional crowd-leading skills.

High school squads are similar to college in that they have a responsibility to be leaders and ambassadors for their schools. They also combine the crowd-leading skills with athleticism to lead their schools in support of its athletic teams.

All Star cheerleading is unique in that it is strictly about performance.

But no matter what level you're at or what type of squad you're on, cheerleaders have been and will continue to be a part of pop culture and the fabric of sports. Of course, there are the stereotypes, but I think television exposure has helped people see that cheerleading definitely involves athleticism and leadership.

Cheerleading continues to evolve and that still gets me excited. Before our camps each year, when I meet with our instructors to talk about the material for the year and their impact, I still get charged up. And when I go to a college football or basketball game, it really makes me proud to see how a team can use its talent and skills to affect the crowd and motivate the team. It's a great thing.

I probably don't reflect on the past often enough—I'm a typical type-A person, and move quickly from one thing to the next. But when I do let myself stop and think, it really amazes me to see how far cheerleading has come in such a short period of time. I think back to that first UCA High School Cheerleading National Championship and the impact it had, and I think, "Wow, that really ushered in the next generation of cheerleading and inspired a nation."

Founder of the Universal Cheerleaders Association (UCA)
Founder, Chairman, and CEO of Varsity Brands, Inc.

Squad: Cheered at the University of Oklahoma
Interesting Fact: For a quarter of a century, Jeff Webb has anchored ESPN's coverage of UCA cheerleading programming. Webb's children have also followed in his athletic footsteps, with son Jeffrey a star soccer player and daughter Caroline a stand-out in track and field and soccer.

CHAPTER 3

You've examined your squad options and decided what's best for you. Now let's figure out how to get you ready for cheerleading tryouts. First step: Don't panic! When you are on the outside looking in, it may seem that everyone else knows exactly what they are doing, and that they are doing it with little effort. Don't be fooled. Everyone started from scratch.

Diligence and persistence during tryouts paid off for these University of Tennessee cheerleaders.

Making

the Team

Get Moving!

To land a spot on the squad, you'll need stamina, strength, and flexibility. So, if you aren't already exercising regularly, the first thing to do is to start! If you wait until tryouts to get into shape, you're likely to overdo it and strain a muscle. If you're trying out for the first time, you should aim to start working out at least four to six weeks before tryouts.

To prepare for cheerleading's long, grueling season—games are long and practices can be even longer—you'll need some serious stamina. To build your stamina, jog or bike a few times each week, and gradually increase the distance you go.

Also consider working on strength-building. Regardless of whether you end up on the bottom of a stunt formation as a base, or on the top as a flyer, you'll need to be strong. If you belong to a gym, then you'll have access to all kinds of machines to work your arms and legs. But you can also incorporate strength-building into your everyday activities, by carrying groceries, younger siblings, and your heavy school bag! If you plan to jog to get in shape, consider taking along small weights to pump as you run.

If you're a newcomer, look for a cheer camp or All Star facility that offers an introduction to cheerleading. If there's no place to learn the basics ahead of time, consider signing up for a gymnastics or dance class. Both will build your flexibility, coordination, and confidence—gymnastics moves are used when cheerleaders tumble, and most cheer squads perform at least one choreographed dance a season as part of their routine.

For many newcomers, the most intimidating part of cheerleading is jumping. It can seem impossible to lift your legs as high as the veterans do, but don't declare defeat until you've practiced for at least a month. Jumping is part strength, part flexibility, and part momentum, so make sure your legs get a regular workout. To improve your flexibility, stretch in both sitting and standing positions. Working with a partner, rest one ankle on her shoulder. As she holds your ankle in place, have her gradually move from a squatting to a standing position. When she reaches your limit, ask her to stop and to hold the position she's in for twenty seconds. Switch legs, then offer to do the same exercise for her. After you've improved your flexibility, you'll feel more comfortable lifting and swinging your legs higher on your own. Swinging your legs will help give your body the momentum it needs for that first proud jump off the floor.

Since many cheer jumps begin from a standing position, you'll also need to practice building your momentum without swinging. Here's a trick from the world of martial arts: Ask a partner to face you with his palms facing up at stomach level, his feet shoulder length apart, and his knees bent for lifting. Place your palms on his, and practice jumps with kicks to the side— not to the front at your partner! As you jump, push down on his palms, and he will push up on yours, to help give you a little lift and keep your torso straight.

You'll need a good deal of strength and flexibility to perform even the most basic jump, a toe touch, so start training early.

In addition to physical fitness, here are some other things you'll need to have in order before tryout time:

▶ **Time** in your schedule for practices, cheer events, and your own training.

▶ **Permission to participate** from your parents if you're under eighteen.

▶ **Grades, course load,** and **age** that meet the organization's requirements.

▶ A **love** and growing passion for cheering, dance, and gymnastics.

During tryouts coaches will often first teach the material in large groups in an effort to identify the quick learners. From there, cheerleaders will break into smaller groups to practice these same skills.

Let's Get Clinical!

Prior to the actual tryout day, most schools hold tryout clinics. Clinics are where you'll learn what you'll actually be asked to perform at tryouts: the cheer, dance routine, jumps, stunts, and tumbling passes. You'll also get the chance to meet veteran cheerleaders and watch them in action. You'll likely be assigned a tryout group. Finally, clinics will teach you the dos and don'ts of tryout day, so there won't be any last-minute surprises.

Clinic Tips:

> Dress in comfortable workout wear, such as a T-shirt, shorts, socks, appropriate undergarments, and supportive shoes. To allow for body movement, you might want to roll up your sleeves or wear a tank top. Wearing school colors is always appropriate.

> Do not wear jewelry, including watches. If you must wear earrings, wear studs.

> Pull your hair out of your face so you can see and be seen.

> Bring bottled water or a sports drink to sip during breaks.

> Mute your cell phone's ringer. Nobody wants to hear ring tones when he or she is concentrating on the dance music.

> Arrive on time—or early. Use spare time to stretch.

▷▷ Practice Makes Perfect

Everybody has to attend the clinics, but nobody is going to force you to practice between the time they end and the actual tryout day. Make rehearsing a top priority during clinic week. Rehearse with an honest friend who will watch your routine and help you correct it. Be sure to do the same for him or her in return.

To help you rehearse, many schools make arrangements for you to get a copy of the music used for the dance routine. Make sure to get that version as it may not be the same version as the one you download to your iPod. Write down all the steps of the dance and cheer. If you have access to a video camera, tape the instructor performing the routine. It's also a good idea to ask a friend to videotape you as you perform the routine. Watching yourself on camera will help you identify what moves need work.

Left: Listening closely during clinics and taking time to work with a coach can help you hone skills and master moves.

Below and right: Partners Brandon Gwynn and Brittany Wilde practice their moves during tryouts for the University of Louisville.

ARRIVE EARLY!

STRETCH PROPERLY!

BE FRIENDLY!

The Big Day

On the day of tryouts, come rested, relaxed, and ready. Familiarize yourself with the tryout room and pay attention to any directions. If everyone remains in the competition room, sit quietly. Do not giggle, talk to the people sitting near you, or react negatively as others are judged. When your name or number is called, jump up and enter the room with spirit, confidence, and enthusiasm!

Show the judges a natural smile and keep smiling, even if you've made a mistake—confidence is often more important than correctness. Project your voice, maintain eye contact with the judges, and don't be shocked if something doesn't go according to plan. If the music player stops playing, keep dancing. If the judges forget to ask your group to do jumps, wait until you've been dismissed then raise your hand and politely remind them.

When it's all over, prepare for the worst, but act your best. If you don't make the team, admitting it to yourself privately will help keep you from crying publicly. Whether or not you make the team, be a good sport. Congratulate your friends who did and show sympathy for those who didn't. Thank the coaches, regardless. Remember, if they need a mid-season replacement, they are more likely to pick someone who left tryouts on a positive note. And besides, there's always next year.

Tryouts can be draining, but an upbeat attitude and a bright outlook will help keep spirits high.

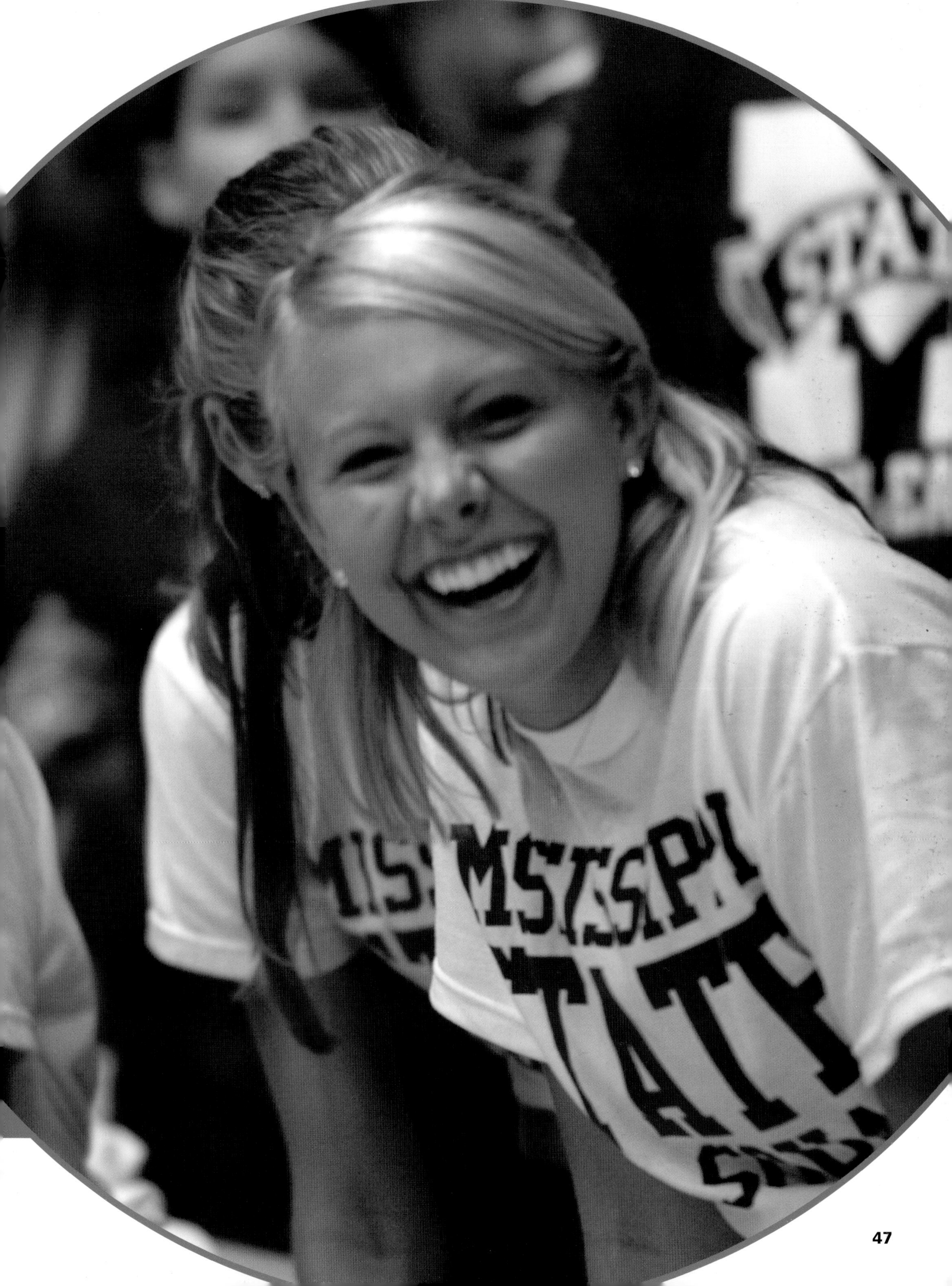

High School Tryouts

Gone are the days when cheerleaders were selected by their classmates in a popularity contest. A Texas school board banned that practice in 1999 and insisted cheerleaders make the squad based on skill, ability, and spirit. Most schools have had skill-based tryouts for decades, though the particular skill expectations vary from school to school and even from squad to squad within the school.

Step One: Pre-Pre-Tryouts

You're exercising. You've completed your cheer application, gotten your parents to sign your liability waiver, had a physical, gathered together any other materials required by your school, and returned all necessary paperwork to the coach. Now you just have to wait for the tryout clinics to start, right?

No you don't! If you have cheerleading friends, make a gym date to review basics from last year. Plan for safety, with mats and plenty of extra spotters. If you're new to the sport, ask a cheerleader you know if you can get together. In talking, you'll find out what the team's last season was like, get the lowdown on the coaches, and pick up some cheerleading lingo. If you meet at the gym, you might even learn a few basic jumps or dance moves. If you just moved to the area and don't know anyone, check the library and/or the Internet for books, CDs, or videos that demonstrate the terms and techniques you'll be learning in a few weeks. Don't try to stunt alone, but do make use of all available resources.

To pump up your enthusiasm along with your technique, add some dance time to your exercise routine. Start off free styling, then pick a song and choreograph it. Some tryouts include a free-style dance segment, and although you may not know in advance the song that will be used, dancing on your own ahead of time is the best preparation for this. If you've been dancing regularly, you're more likely to show a greater range of moves, display better body control, and exude more confidence. As you practice, smile and maintain eye contact with your imaginary audience—a mirror or bookshelf will do.

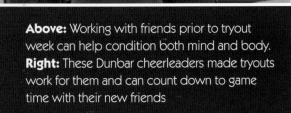

Above: Working with friends prior to tryout week can help condition both mind and body.
Right: These Dunbar cheerleaders made tryouts work for them and can count down to game time with their new friends

CHAMPIONSHIPS

Before tryouts, find out whether your squad competes or if it solely supports your athletic teams. Skills required for tryouts can vary.

Step Two: Pre-Tryouts

The first time you show up at your new high school's tryout clinics and look over a sea of cheerleading candidates, you might wonder, "Who ARE all these people?" The massive group can generally be divided into three categories: the veteran cheerleaders from your school, cheerleaders from feeder schools, and those new to the sport. As the squad will likely end up containing people from all three of these groups, it's to everyone's advantage to get along and work together gracefully.

Since people are arriving with varying levels of cheer knowledge and from locations where different terminology may have been used, the coach will probably spend quite a bit of time explaining things, particularly the first day. Even if you have cheered all your life, pay attention, and keep your eyes on the coach. There may be changes you weren't expecting, and the coach will appreciate your respect.

The first few drills will probably be crafted for beginners. If that's you, try your best. If you're a veteran, stay focused and put the "leader" back in "cheerleader." Instead of pointing out the people who can't lift their feet past their knees, offer sincere encouragement and assistance, especially to those just starting out. If the coach allows stretching and practicing in line, set a good example. Partner with a new person and help him or her master the steps.

When put into stunting groups, it can be tempting to show off—particularly if you're in an all-veteran-varsity group and everyone's practicing elevators. But before you start basket tossing, check with the coach. It may be that you are needed to provide additional spotters on the mats for the less experienced groups. Jumping

> A Typical High School Tryout

Cheer Coach Cari Merson of Edison High School in Alexandria, Virginia, says about 75 percent of the people who try out at her school make one of the three squads. "For the varsity squad, we want to make sure everyone has a standing back handspring, at least with a spot; ability to do double jumps; and have level jumps, strong stunting skills, sharp motions, strong dance skills, spirit, and enthusiasm. For junior varsity we expect strong motions, decent dance skills, decent jumps, spirit, and enthusiasm. To make the freshman squad, we look for willingness and potential to learn cheer skills."

Before the actual tryouts, Merson organizes two to three days of cheer clinics. She introduces her assistants and provides each applicant with a numbered sticker. Before beginning the formal clinic, the assistants lead the candidates through basic stretching exercises. Jumps are demonstrated, then applicants—in groups of four—practice them. After a break, the candidates learn a short dance routine. They rotate position on the floor so that everyone has the opportunity to be close to the instructor and to have a good view. After a second break, Merson discusses safe stunting and the value of spotters. Stunting groups are assigned to practice an elevator.

While potential cheerleaders are learning what it takes to be an Edison cheerleader, Merson and her assistants are learning about the candidates. They notice which veterans are helping newcomers, who seems distracted and who is paying attention, which candidates spend downtime stretching or practicing their new moves, and who helps to clean up the gym afterward without being asked. "Anyone can learn to jump, dance, and smile. What we love to see are true leaders." Often the people who assist at the clinics are also judges at the actual tryout. When scores are close, the experience of working with the potential cheerleaders during the clinics becomes extremely valuable. Recently, Merson assigned a newcomer to the varsity squad, which upset some of the veterans. But Merson saw the newcomer making an extra effort during the tryout clinics. She said this new girl quickly caught up to her varsity teammates, surprising the doubters.

straight into an advanced stunt could distract others and prevent them from learning what they need to know, and be unnecessarily intimidating. At some point, the coach may separate potential varsity cheerleaders from the rest to review advanced skills. That's when it's most appropriate to practice the higher-level moves.

Step Three: Tryouts

The big day arrives. Hopefully you've had a good sleep and did not spend the whole night practicing!

Wash your hair, style it according to the coach's instructions, and check your gym bag to make sure you have any necessary ID, a sports drink, a spare outfit (in case something happens to the one you are wearing), any notes you want to review before tryouts, and your cell phone—ringer off! If it's an all-day tryout, be sure to include some nutritious snacks and a light lunch.

Give yourself plenty of time to get there, and aim to arrive early. Scope the layout. Imagine yourself executing a perfect performance in the space designated, or—better yet—if you're allowed, practice the routines in these new surroundings ahead of time. Smile, greet the other candidates, and be sure of yourself.

When the coach provides last-minute instructions, pay attention. As applicants try out and return to the hallway, they're going to be excited and maybe even scared, so try not to hang on their every word—it will just make you more nervous.

▷ Choosing a Captain

The ideal cheer captain is fair and dependable, a person who gets along well with the coach and teammates. If the candidates for captain are given a chance to speak to your team, listen to their campaign talks and be wary of extravagant promises. It's best to elect someone who will follow through with commitments, as opposed to someone who exaggerates and then drops the ball. If your squad elects co-captains, select people who work together well and who'll help each other as needed. It's important the co-captains respect each other as well as their teammates.

If you are a newcomer to the squad, base your vote on how people behaved during the tryout clinics. Who helped newcomers learn the routines? Who was "all talk" and who was "all action"?

Don't be surprised when others ask who you're planning to vote for. If you aren't sure, say so. Ask their opinions. If you have a strong opinion, you can state your reasons, but be careful about offending any of the other candidates. If you're nervous about getting involved in a popularity contest or are undecided, you can say,

"I'm trying to figure out who will be the best leader for our squad—who seems fair, and dependable, and able to work well with everyone else."

And if the coach decides who should be captain, don't be offended. The coach may recognize someone's leadership abilities based on previous experience more quickly than the squad does, or the coach may want to keep the squad from starting off the year with an overly politicized fight.

When choosing a captain, skill level is important, but make sure to consider character and dependability as well.

The All Star Factor

Unlike tryouts for school teams—where the competition to make the squad can be stiff—tryouts for All Star squads are usually focused on grouping candidates into appropriate teams by talent level. At the end of each All Star season, entire squads are re-evaluated to determine if the squad as a whole is ready to advance to the next level. In some cases individual cheerleaders are shuffled to a new team, one that better matches his or her skill level. Since most All Star centers field several teams categorized by age and skill level, it's rare for someone not to make a team at all.

Another difference from high school cheerleading is the emphasis on skills, such as dancing and tumbling, over actual cheers. While high school cheerleaders are usually on the sidelines, cheering for football and basketball teams, All Star cheerleaders focus on competitive routines using dancing, tumbling, and stunting. This is where years of gymnastics and dance lessons prove particularly helpful.

Probably the biggest difference between All Star tryouts and other cheer tryouts is that many All Star facilities will allow newcomers to schedule personal tryouts with the facility coaches if they have moved into the area past the official tryout date. In fact some All Star programs have a class specifically designed for newcomers to cheerleading. This class introduces them to basic skills and helps the coaches evaluate which squad would be the most appropriate. These classes are generally offered year-round and can include stretching and flexibility, back-handspring instruction, and even cartwheel classes for the younger group. The instructional classes progress by level, beginning with back tucks and layouts, and eventually moving to twists and more advanced skills.

At All Star tryouts, cheerleaders are evaluated for their performance skills and technique level, instead of how well they cheer and chant.

> Tryouts, Elite Style

Kentucky Elite, an All Star program out of Lexington, holds a three- to four-week sign-up period before tryout clinics begin. This period gives candidates plenty of time to complete and return paperwork. Brian Elza from Kentucky Elite advises candidates to be prepared: "Read the packet of information; it explains the year. Make sure parents are aware of the schedule and costs, and that everyone knows what to expect."

The tryouts at Kentucky Elite are closed—no spectators are allowed. Usually four coaches, who serve as judges at the tryouts, select teams based on skill level and age. The judges may decide to place a cheerleader with exceptional ability on a more advanced team than what might be usual for someone of his or her age. Thirty minutes after tryouts conclude, team rosters are posted and a meeting for parents is held.

Over the course of one week, candidates attend two to three clinics, each lasting about ninety minutes. They learn what they'll need to demonstrate at tryouts and are taught a cheer and a dance. As Elza explains, "We don't want to overwhelm the participants. We want to see that they'll go home, practice what they've been shown, and come back stronger the next day." The official tryouts are usually held a day or two after the clinics end.

Since All Star participants range in age, younger kids and newcomers to the sport are not expected to have much cheer background. But older applicants do usually demonstrate some training in dance or tumbling. The judges design their scorecards to replicate the criteria their teams will face in competitions. They build the teams from top to bottom, generally selecting seven to nine tops per team and then the appropriate number of bases and back spots.

College Tryouts

While you are learning about a college's cheer program, you'll also want to find out the details of when tryouts will be held. Some schools hold tryouts in the spring, expecting incoming students to either show up for tryouts or send the coaching staff a tryout video. Other schools hold tryouts in the early fall, close to the beginning of the school year. Still others have a mixed tryout, with the main tryout in the spring and a smaller one, aimed at recruiting freshmen (if there are open spots available) in the fall.

The paperwork associated with cheerleading tryouts doesn't end when you go to college. Schools expect you to show proof you are or will be a student in good standing, proof of medical insurance and, if you're under 18, permission from your parents to participate. In addition, you may be asked for recent transcripts, proof you've had a physical, and/or recommendation letters from previous coaches. Since each school will have its own list of requirements, be sure to read any distributed material carefully.

Left and above: From clothes to practices and paperwork, colleges vary widely in their tryout requirements.
Right: Prior to college tryouts, take time to learn the squad's competitive history and the school's traditions.

Do Your Homework

Do an Internet search on your college cheer squad and find out about its recent competitions. Check to see what competitions the team participated in, and how they performed. You can also talk to people who cheered in that competition, including the squad veterans. How much time was spent on stunts versus on dance? How was tumbling incorporated? What were the team's favorite parts of the routine? You can also ask about where they fell short, as long as you're tactful and non-threatening in your questioning.

Once you've got some background information, look for ways you can add value to the team. Perhaps the team was rated poorly for choreography in last year's competition, and you choreographed several routines for your old squad. Should this be the case, be sure to find a way to squeeze such valuable information onto the application form and be prepared to answer questions about your choreography experience during official interviews and/or unofficial chats with coaches. If possible, tuck a video of your old squad performing

your stellar routine into your gym bag, just in case the coach asks to see it. But again, tact is crucial—the person with whom you are talking could in fact be the one responsible for the poor choreography!

> Professional Tryouts: Beyond the Moves

Tryouts at the professional sports level are drastically different from tryouts at all the other stages of cheerleading. For starters, hundreds of people try out for each professional cheer team each year, including the squad's veterans who have to try out all over again every year. A typical professional tryout process will consist of up to five rounds, and will include several rounds of cuts, and an interview. Some teams keep the entire audition process away from prying eyes, behind locked doors. Others put potential cheerleaders in front of a realistic audience for the final round.

When Wanda Brown, director and choreographer of the Washington Wizards Dance Team, looks at candidates, she tries to find dancers who will appeal to the whole crowd. "We're not looking for sexy; we want dancers who will hold the attention of the kids and older fans with their showmanship and charisma. Dance is important, but we want to find people with something more." That's why she diversifies her panel of judges. She includes some with dance backgrounds, some from the Wizards' office without dance backgrounds, a player, and one guest judge (such as a local news reporter). While over one hundred applicants try out, only twenty make the squad.

"From Gymnastics to Cheerleading"

I had been raised to believe that cheerleading was a hobby for wimps and that it would lead me nowhere. I'm so glad I decided to ignore that and was able to discover the sport that would take me from high school and All Star cheerleading, through college and into my career.

When I was a kid, gymnastics was my life. My two older sisters were involved in gymnastics, and as soon as I understood what forward rolls and cartwheels were, I started to try them myself. That was when my parents decided it would be best for me to practice these moves in the safe, structured environment of a gym. For the next ten years I lived and breathed gymnastics. I had goals though, and one of them was to make it to the Junior Olympic Nationals as a level ten, which I reached at the end of seventh grade. Despite everyone's concern that I would regret it, I immediately retired from gymnastics. I will admit that now and then, I still think about what might have been. Fortunately for me, I found cheerleading soon after leaving gymnastics.

My cheerleading career started with my first school tryouts. In order to participate, I had to attend a clinic held by the previous year's cheerleaders. The first three days of the clinic we learned all the material we would need to know for the tryout. After that, there was a full run-through to prepare us for what to do in front of the judges. At the real tryouts, we had to go out one by one and perform in front of the judges, then two other girls joined in to do a cheer and a dance. The final day of tryouts was held in front of the student body. This was probably the most nerve-wracking experience of my life—even more than Junior Olympic Nationals! The entire student body watched and then voted for the people they wanted to represent the school. As you can probably imagine, this setup had the tendency to turn the tryouts into a popularity contest.

I honestly did not even think of cheering in college until my senior year in high school. I was participating in different competitions with my All Star squad, and watching coaches from different colleges talk to my teammates about coming to their schools and receiving scholarships. While this sounded exciting to me, I still wasn't sold on the idea because I thought I already knew where I was headed for college. But my perspective changed when the college coaches began telling me about what their schools had to offer. This is when I decided I would listen, in case there was something worth considering.

By January of my senior year I had been convinced to try out at the University of Kentucky. I went to Lexington guarded. Kentucky was the strongest team in the nation and I didn't want to be upset if I didn't make the team. After a week of clinics and an extraordinarily long day of tryouts, I made the blue squad, which entitled me to a full scholarship.

Looking back over the past ten years I cannot imagine not being involved in cheerleading. I started off not knowing anything except that cheerleading involved tumbling and a lot of flexibility and coordination, all things which I knew that I would want to keep up from my gymnastics career. And now, here I am, having cheered for my high school, All Stars, and college. Cheerleading has helped me understand who I am and what I'm worth, two things for which I'll be forever grateful.

Squads: University of Kentucky; CMC All Stars (Mississippi); Jackson Preparatory School
Hometown: Flowood, MS
Interesting Fact: Sara was a three-time national champion with the University of Kentucky and an individual collegiate partner-stunt national champion.

CHAPTER 4

Tryouts are over, the squads have been selected, and you've made the cut! (Breathe!) But don't count on relaxing too much. Cheerleading camp is on the horizon, and you'll only get out of it what you put into it. Look at it this way: Camp is a perfect time to break out of your comfort zone. It can help you improve your individual technique and make your team work together better. A good camp fosters squad unity and team training as well as individual advancements in stunting, jumping, dance, and crowd leading.

You and your teammates will develop strong bonds—and lasting memories—each summer at cheerleading camp.

Gone

Camping!

These days squad members put their heads together to decide their destiny for summer camp.

Choose Your Adventure

You'll get the most out of your summer experience if you choose the right camp. From commuter to residential, day to overnight, the range of camps available is extensive. Plus, not all programs are taught at the same pace. Instruction at some is general and relaxed, while at others it may be more rigorous or specialized in focus. All Star squads may choose to go to an All Star-specific camp (which focuses more on performance and less on crowd leading), or stay closer to home and participate in a private camp at their gym.

While in the past, cheer coaches and/or advisors often made the decision about what type of camp their squad should attend, the current trend is for the coach, advisor, and their cheerleaders to make this decision together. Also, many squads are choosing to attend multiple camps, each one with a different focus—such as a skills camp followed by a choreography camp. Most camps last about five days.

When considering which camp to attend, you and your team must first figure out what you hope to gain from the experience. If your main goal is to bond as a group and find some new, fresh routines to bring home, you'll want to choose a residential cheer camp. If you're mainly focused on improving your stunting skills, you'll want to look into a stunt-specific camp. Or, if you want to learn more about combining stunting with tumbling, a number of stunt and tumbling camps are offered.

Next, you'll need to evaluate your skill level. What are your team's strengths and weaknesses? Are the majority of you new to cheerleading or have you been cheering for a while? Do you want a "business-only" experience or do you want to have some fun outside of cheering? The answers to these questions will help you determine the type of camp that will be best for you and your squad.

▶ What to Expect at Camp

Most camps group squads based on the age of their participants. And they usually offer programs in the following divisions: youth, junior high, high school, college prep, and college.

If you're overwhelmed by the number of camps to choose from, here's a cheat sheet that may help:

Where Do You Live?

> **RESIDENTIAL**
- Traditionally held at college campuses. These programs often utilize the school's cafeteria and dorm rooms. Cheerleaders stay overnight.

> **COMMUTER**
- Can be held at any facility. Cheerleaders don't stay overnight.

What Do You Learn?

> **CHEER CAMPS**
- Learn game cheers, chants, and dances, and even develop a pep-rally routine to bring back to your own school. Get tips and techniques for crowd leading from the sidelines.
- Learn stunt techniques while perfecting jumps and other movements.
- These camps are generally held at college campuses and last between four and five days.
- A daily spirit award is given.
- Various competitions are held.

> **STUNT CAMPS**
- Focus solely on creative stunts: pyramids, basket sequences, and more.
- Seminars may be held.
- Programs generally last two to three days.

> **CHOREOGRAPHY CAMPS**
- Develop creative routines for your squad.
- These camps may include dance and music instruction.
- Programs range from two days to a week, depending upon the type of choreography being taught.

> **STUNT & TUMBLE CAMPS**
- Typically held at a facility with a tumble track, spring floor, and trampoline.
- Program length varies.

Additional Varieties

> **RESORT CAMPS**
- Usually held at a beach or lake setting.
- Program includes fun activities on the beach, dance parties at night, and beach time during the day!

> **CHRISTIAN CAMPS**
- Program includes bible study and prayer time as well as activities to facilitate spiritual growth.

> **PRIVATE**
- Typically held by All Star gyms for their squads; programs are open only to members of the gym's teams.
- The schedule is based upon the coach's needs and goals.
- Depending upon demand, programs can be as short as half a day.
- Companies such as the UCA are now holding private camps (half-day or day), in an effort to give cheerleading squads the chance to jump-start their skills.

> **NON-BUILDING**
- For teams that do not stunt, the focus is on dance and tumbling instruction.
- These programs are held at a host school or All Star gym.

Camp style is comfortable and casual.

Choose camp gear wisely and make sure it's appropriate for the camp you're headed for.

Camp Survival Kit

One of the biggest mistakes you can make occurs before you even arrive at camp: packing the wrong things. Having the right gear will keep you focused on learning and having fun—instead of on the sunburn you'll get because you forgot your sunscreen!

Here's what you need to bring:

 Comfortable cheer shoes (a backup pair is a good idea), shorts, and T-shirts are a must! Bring plenty of workout gear.

 Your everyday toiletries.

Towels and flip-flops for the shower.

 A warm blanket, a pillow, and anything else that will help you rest better after a long day of hard work. Think comfort!

Sunscreen, bug repellant, and plenty of water and snacks to replenish your energy.

 Arts-and-crafts supplies for decorating your door—a great way to showcase your spirit!

Be prepared to incorporate your squad's identity—such as school colors and traditional cheers—into the materials you're taught at camp.

▶ Making the Most of Camp

Regardless of the kind (or kinds) of camps your team decides to attend, it's ultimately up to you and your team to take full advantage of what the program has to offer. While you'll have instructors to guide you, and your coach and teammates will be there, ultimately, you determine what you take from the experience. And what you take from camp can determine your success in the year to follow.

Not all the components of summer camp are technical. Camp is also about trying new things, meeting new people, learning from new instructors, and pushing your limits as an individual and as a team. Here are some non-physical skills to keep in mind while you're there:

Sportsmanship

Camp is a place to practice being a good sport—a graceful winner and loser. Be sure to maintain a positive attitude and willingness to learn when you're working in a different environment than the one you're used to. People will likely take notice of your eagerness and the positive influence your attitude has on those around you. Enthusiasm is contagious!

Cheerleaders look forward to bonding with teammates and partners while learning and perfecting new skills.

Leadership

Take advantage of this opportunity to hone your leadership skills. After all, you'll be surrounded by some of the sharpest leaders around, and these skills are ones that will help you outside of cheerleading, throughout your life. Whether you have an assigned leadership role on your squad or you choose to take on a leadership role at camp (such as helping teammates or even other teams), the ability to truly lead and have a positive impact is not as easy as it looks. Be patient, help others, and guide your friends.

Eagerness

Demonstrate your desire to learn and absorb everything the instructors have to teach you. Be responsive when they ask questions; don't be shy and wait for others to answer. Ask questions yourself and offer suggestions you think may be beneficial to yourself and to those around you.

Spirit

At the heart of every cheerleader is spirit! Let yours shine through at camp. Smile, laugh, and enjoy yourself. Happiness will exude from you if you let it! (P.S.: If enough of your squad members share their spirit, too, your team may win the spirit stick!)

All in a Day's Work

Every day at camp will be a mixture of hard work, sun and fun, team bonding, and individual improvement. While daily schedules vary greatly from one camp to another, there are key elements that will be a part of every camp experience. From early morning roll calls to skills classes to group dinners, you'll likely be on the go from dusk 'til dawn! Here's a look at a typical camp day:

> MORNING

7:15 a.m. BZZZZ! & Breakfast
Yes, that's the sound of your alarm clock going off. Up and at 'em! And don't even think of skipping breakfast—you're going to need your strength!

8:15 a.m. Stretch and Jog
A light jog and stretching will loosen up your muscles for the day ahead.

8:30 a.m. Jump Class
A jump class will have you perfecting your toe touches and pike jumps!

9:00 a.m. Team Time
Now that you're definitely awake, an ice-breaking session will help you bond with your teammates.

10:00 a.m. Stunts
Skill sessions will teach you new stunts to give your routine just the pizzazz it needs!

11:00 a.m. Cheer Class
Here you'll pick up brand-new ways to fire up your crowd for Friday night football.

> AFTERNOON

12:00 p.m. Chow Time!
You've no doubt worked up an appetite. Lunch could not come soon enough!

1:30 p.m. One-on-One
While your morning sessions may have been group sessions with cheerleaders from other squads across the country, the afternoon is all about your team. Instructors will work with squads and individuals to customize routine elements and help perfect skills.

4:30 p.m. Break Time!
You may be in need of a quick power nap after a busy day, but don't plan on being down for long. There is still much more ahead!

> EVENING

6:00 p.m. Come and Get It!
Dinner gives you another opportunity to get tight with teammates and visit with cheerleaders from other squads.

7:00 p.m. How Did I Do?
During the day, camp instructors may have evaluated you and your team. They'll likely use this evening hour to sit down with you to discuss your team's strengths and weaknesses. Regardless of what they say, consider everything in a positive light—the only way to grow is to face new challenges head-on.

8:00 p.m. Dance, Dance!
Finally, a little social time! Camps often plan group activities for the evening to give you a chance to let your hair down, relax, and unwind. From board games to dances to ice-cream socials, enjoy this time to recharge your batteries.

10:00 p.m. Lights Out!
It's time to hit the sack and get some serious rest so you'll be ready to give it your all again tomorrow!

Panama City Beach Resort campers try a different kind of pyramid while having fun in the sun.

▷ Can You Hear the Waves?

In recent years, variations on the traditional camp have evolved so that campers get an experience that resembles a vacation as much as a learning experience. One such option is Universal Cheerleaders Association's Panama City Beach "Resort" camp. Held at the luxurious Edgewater Beach Resort and Conference Center, campers get instruction at an indoor fifteen-thousand-square-foot conference center and moments later head out to the sandy white beaches of Panama City to soak in the sun and surf.

Posh Accomodations

After a long day of hard work, campers have the luxury of retiring to condos equipped with washers and dryers and fully furnished kitchens. Campers are also housed in villas that sleep six. Fancy a slumber party, anyone?

Surf's up!

If you attend this UCA "beach camp," you'll have many entertainment options during downtime. A disc jockey will play favorite tunes while you compete in a limbo contest, play a game of beach volleyball, swim in the pool, or ride the waves. And don't forget your grass skirt and lei. One evening's activity is a luau. It's the shortest flight to Hawaii you'll ever take!

"My Summer Camp Experiences"

Waking up early, losing my voice, and late-night gossip sessions with the girls are all part of my past camp experiences! Every team I have ever cheered with has gone to a UCA camp, and I have attended ones in Georgia, Tennessee, Alabama, North Carolina, Florida, and Kentucky, all of which were unforgettable!

I first went to camp when I was seven years old in North Carolina. I remember my mom was scared to let me go so far away when I was still so young. Because I was the youngest girl on the team, I roomed with older girls, and I thought I was so cool! During the day it was HOT, but it always seems to be hot when you have to stand outside for hours at a time! We learned many cheers and sidelines, but my favorite part of camp was learning the dances! I loved to show off and dance with those older girls. At night, the girls would let me stay up late with them. They would dress me up in their clothes, fix my hair, and put makeup on me. It was one of the best times I have ever had! I will never forget my teammates my very first year, because of how we bonded at camp.

My favorite camp experiences come from high school. My freshman year I went to camp at the University of Kentucky. The days were hot, the food was gross, the nights were exciting, and the memories are priceless. Freshman year for most girls is a time to meet the new girls in your grade, the coaches, and, of course, the big, bad seniors! Freshman year for me was all about acting as normal as possible, even though my mom was the head coach!

Sophomore year we went to Jekyll Island in Georgia—a camp on the beach! Some parents and coaches thought being at the beach might distract us from learning anything new, but it actually made our team closer. It felt like we were all going on a trip together, except that this vacation wasn't all about the beach. We still had to wake up early to learn new stunts, cheers, and dances. We did get some free time, though mine was cut short because of a jellyfish sting!

Junior year we went back to the beach because the year before was such a success. We ended up in Gulf Shores, Alabama. We stayed in condos housing about eight girls each. It was wonderful to wake up and look out at the ocean, and to have camp near the sandy shores! Junior year is also when you realize that you are an older girl on the team and that the younger ones are looking up to you, trying to figure out their places on the squad.

Camp is where each season begins. It's the very first time you come together as a team in your new season. It's where you learn new cheers to use at your football games. It's where leaders are established and friendships are made. This past year, I also feel like I became a lot closer with the girls in my grade. We were friends before, but at camp, secrets are shared, stories are told, and the bond is formed.

Squad: Dunbar High School
Hometown: Lexington, KY
Interesting Fact: Appeared in the Lifetime Television reality series *Cheerleader Nation*

CHAPTER 5

Putting together a strong routine is most often the responsibility of the coach or the head cheerleader. Over time, the more senior cheerleaders on a team may also earn the right to serve as choreographers. Planning a routine takes extra time, something that in most cases, cheerleaders don't have a lot of. But when your squad pulls off a successful performance, it's well worth the effort. So if you are interested in learning how to choreograph, speak up! There may be opportunities for you to watch and learn.

River Cities demonstrates its ability to put a fully choreographed and perfected routine together at the 2006 World Championships of All Star Cheerleading.

Anything

CHAMPIONSHIP OF ALL STAR CHEERLEADING

but Routine!

Before the music starts, nerves, anxiety, excitement, and anticipation need to be harnessed so that a routine can be executed to perfection.

The Magic Mix: Elements of a Routine

As a choreographer works to piece together a routine, there are certain key components to keep in mind:

Music: Music can make or break a routine, so be sure the song you choose sounds professional and complements your moves. For example, you wouldn't want the words "falling down" to be sung as your team is building a pyramid! Sound effects can be great, but be careful of going overboard. Also, make sure the music isn't too slow—cheerleading routines are most entertaining when they are energetic and fast paced.

Cheer: If you want the crowd's participation, keep your cheering clean and crisp. Avoid having too much going on at once as that may confuse and distract the fans, causing them to forget to cheer along with you.

Dance: When choreographing a dance, you'll want to avoid inappropriate gestures. In recent years, teams have been penalized for suggestive moves, both at sporting events and in official cheerleading competitions. A dance looks best when there is strong formation and level changes. Of course synchronization, timing, sharpness, and appropriate facial expressions are a must! And again, the presentation as a whole is most effective and fun when the dance complements the music.

Tumbling: When competing, it's necessary to assess how many tumblers are realistically able to perform each type of pass. Remember: Don't show what you don't have! You will lose more points for falling than you will for going with—and successfully landing—a simpler pass. Also, step in time with the music and be sure to choreograph moves at appropriate spots. Back handsprings and back tucks are two of the most common tumbling passes used in cheering today.

Stunts/Pyramids: As in tumbling, the degree of difficulty of the stunts you choose to include in a routine should be weighed against how successful the team is at performing them. For instance, if you perform a routine that includes more difficult moves, but the team has a weak performance with many drops and shakes, you will lose points in difficulty, execution, and overall effect. However, if you perform a routine with simpler moves, but the performance is perfect, you will only lose points in difficulty. Thus, your team will be awarded a higher score than it would have been had you attempted—and unsuccessfully performed—a harder routine. Even at school, fans are generally more receptive to and appreciative of a clean, smooth routine.

Formation/Spacing: Routines are easier to perform—not to mention better looking—when the formation changes are free of "traffic jams." Using choreographed arm motions in between moves can ensure the continuous flow of a routine. When executed correctly, this type of change can be impressive. But a word to the wise: Be careful. Too many arm moves—or overly complicated ones—can look sloppy. Sometimes just keeping things simple is best! If you have a smaller team, you can actually make it look larger by adding more space between cheerleaders in dance and jump formations. Both a variety of formations and spacing will add visual appeal to your routine.

Jumps: How many different jumps can your team execute? The new trend is to perform many jumps in a row. So, if you are talented jumpers, show off your skills! Make sure everyone's arms are in line, legs are high, toes are pointed, and that synchronization is perfect. Incorporating dance and formation changes will make the overall effect impressive. And don't forget, you can tumble out of jumps as well! Today's most popular jumps include toe touches, pikes, and Herkies.

Flow: The best choreographers know how to create a routine that flows smoothly, from start to finish, without any choppy breaks. Smooth flow is crucial to the success of both competitive and school cheering routines. While both contain similar elements, school routines are less elaborate and generally shorter. But in either case, a smooth start sets the tone for the entire performance. Here is an example of a well-flowing routine:

1. Begin with motion dance

2. Transition to pyramid

3. Move to jump sequence using formation and level changes; incorporate standing tumbling

4. Transition to stunt sequence and second motion dance

5. Move to cross tumbling section; follow with dynamic, high-energy dance segment

6. End with transitional stunt sequence leading to pyramid!

Routine for Routines

There is no ideal routine in cheerleading except that your choreography should reflect whom or what you are cheering for. If your team is performing at a game or pep rally, you'll want a clean, simple, fun routine—perhaps 10 eight-counts of dance and 5 eight-counts of movement at the end to get into position to perform a transitional pyramid. However, if your team is competing, you should include more difficult moves. You'll need to have a two-and-a-half-minute routine packed with tumbling, jumps, dancing, stunts, and motions. But either way, no matter what your focus, once you have set your goals, you should remember the following:

 Shoot for Success.

Make sure you are realistic about the level of skill required to perform your routine. You want to challenge your team enough to keep them interested, but the moves must be within their reach. Be sure to set yourselves up for success!

 Choreograph Accordingly.

Is your team performing for judges at a competition or performing for alumni, the student body, and fans at a game or pep rally? The answer to this question will dictate how your routine should be choreographed. If you're planning for a competition, you'll need a copy of that particular competition's rules and guidelines in order to develop a routine that will earn as many points as possible. (See example score sheet on page 81.) If you're planning for an event that involves crowd leading, you'll want to be sure to incorporate props (such as signs and pompons) and cheers that encourage the crowd to chant along. After all, nothing beats raving fans!

Style to Suit.

Be sure to keep your team's strengths and weaknesses in mind. Again, a common mistake is to create a routine that is too difficult. If your group is weak in tumbling but strong in stunting, incorporate more stunting than tumbling. (Just remember that for competitions, you must give your team the opportunity to demonstrate all the skills required to earn points.) For crowd leading, plan a routine that is clean and simple. There's no need to stress your team out by asking them to do something they are not yet capable of doing. After all, entertaining at a game or pep rally is meant to be fun, not embarrassing! And since your team isn't competing, there's no need to risk looking sloppy or having someone get hurt for the sake of a too-difficult stunt. Besides, fans won't remember if the team does a straight-up liberty verses a full-up liberty. But they will remember if the liberty drops or looks shaky.

Words to Cheer By

What's the cheer edict for the future? Don't perform a skill if you can't perform it perfectly! While in the past, polish and presentation were not as important, today it's considered crucial to have a solid foundation of skills upon which to build. It's not so much whether you can do a certain tumbling pass or stunt that counts, but rather how well you do the tumbling passes and stunts you are able to do. Ask yourself the following questions: Are your toes pointed? Is your chest up? Are your legs together? Did you set up your back tuck properly? Did you complete the full twist? Remember, the key is basics, basics, basics! Precision, precision, precision! These two words can't be said enough!

Eyes and Ears

Now that you've determined *why* and *what* you're performing, let's discuss *how* you'll do it. First, consider what spectators like to see and hear. For half-time and pep-rally performances, themes are a great idea. You can spice things up by incorporating props that complement the music. Spectators at a game are more apt to sing along with popular songs, while a crowd at a cheering competition will most likely be more interested in your overall performance. Cheer mixes can be great for competitive or non-competitive routines. However, be careful not to use too many. That can make for a choppy, disjointed routine. A general rule of thumb is no more than one song per eight-count!

Crowd Leading's Greatest Hits:

1 A take off of the movie *Grease*

2 A performance in the spirit of a specific decade such as the '70s or '80s

3 Anything Elvis!

4 A performance inspired by a current movie or TV show

AMPIONSHIPS

2006

SPIRIT

Secret

Propel
FITNESS WATER

ESPN

VARSITY

UDA

NIKE

Practice makes perfect for the University of Kentucky. The team works to perfect skills like this pike split-full before UCA's College National Championships.

You Be the Judge: Competitive Cheer

What do judges *really* look for? To get an idea, look over some sample score sheets, like the one on the facing page.

In general, your routine should flow smoothly and be well paced. You don't want too many things going on at the same time—that's a recipe for chaos. But conversely, if there's not enough going on, or if the routine is simply too slow, both the judges and your audience may end up bored. You'll want to be sure to pace your display of skills in an even way. Packing too much into one section may cause the judges and audience to miss something important.

Routines used to be all about the so-called "happy medium." But over time, choreographers went into overdrive, incorporating excessive music cuts, talking over the music, and having way too many transitions. At this point, they have come to realize simpler, cleaner routines can be jam-packed with difficulty and are more fun to watch. Like anything else, there's a balance to good choreography. And as with many things, one of the best ways to learn is to keep an eye on the experts!

E is for Execution

When you've got all your key elements in place, the final step—the finishing touch—is the execution. Walk through your routine slowly and take stock of what you've created:

☐ Does the synchronization work?

☐ How is the team's technique in performing the skills? Is it shaky or does each person hit each move solidly?

☐ Do team members look like they're having fun or do they look bored or stressed out?

☐ Details count: Are the jumps high? Are everyone's toes pointed and arms swinging together?

Judges may also award points for difficulty. How these points are awarded depends upon the level of the team. For example, if your team is signed up to compete in a level-5 competition, and the hardest stunts and pyramids you choreograph are considered level 4 in difficulty, then you probably won't earn full points for difficulty, which will ultimately lower your score. So be sure to know what the level rules and criteria are for the particular competition you have entered.

A final word of advice for choreographers: Your routine should start off high energy and end even higher. Don't let those judges or fans take their eyes off of your squad for even a second!

Judges love watching routines that captivate throughout the entire performance (**above**). But if routines distract judges from the main skills, this can affect scores. Keep routines clean and on the right skill level by reviewing score sheets in advance (**right**).

jamfest! JAMFEST SCORE SHEET jamfest!
cheer and dance events — cheer and dance events

Entry Name ___ Division ___ City/State ___

Event Name ___ Event Date ___ Event City/State ___

CATEGORY	MAX	PTS.	COMMENTS	
Partner Stunts	10		☐ Good Stunts ☐ Clean Dismounts ☐ Good Stunt Incorporation	☐ Stunts Not Steady ☐ Sloppy Cradles ☐ Timing Off
Pyramids/Tosses	10		☐ Good Height on Tosses ☐ Good Pyramids ☐ Good Variation	☐ Tosses Need More Height ☐ Stronger in Air
Running Tumbling	10		☐ Strong Tumbling ☐ Good Incorporation ☐ Good Squad Tumbling	☐ Needs To Be Stronger ☐ Tumbling Off ☐ Needs More Squad Tumbling
Standing Tumbling	10		☐ Strong Tumbling ☐ Good Incorporation ☐ Good Squad Tumbling	☐ Needs To Be Stronger ☐ Tumbling Off ☐ Needs More Squad Tumbling
Jumps	10		☐ Good Jump Incorporation ☐ Good Variety ☐ Good Precision ☐ Good Jumps/Height	☐ Point Toes ☐ Jumps Need Variety ☐ More Height on Jumps ☐ Jumps Off
Motion/Dance Technique	10		☐ Strong Motions ☐ Good Variety of Motions ☐ Flashy/Exciting ☐ Good Incorporation ☐ Good Movements/Motions	☐ Flying Arms/Bent Wrists ☐ Needs Variety ☐ Not Together ☐ Too Fast/ Too Slow ☐ Add Difficulty
Spacing/Transitions/Synchronization	10		☐ Good Use of Floor ☐ Good Spacing ☐ Good Variety of Formations ☐ Smooth Transitions ☐ Good Timing	☐ Watch Spacing ☐ Formations Need Variety ☐ Use More of the Floor ☐ Transitions Sloppy ☐ Not Together
Choreography/Creativity/Flow	10		☐ Solid Routine ☐ Very Creative ☐ Good Use of Skills ☐ Good Flow	☐ Choppy/Doesn't Flow ☐ Too Much/Jumbled ☐ Too Fast/Too Slow
Degree of Difficulty	10		☐ Good Difficulty	☐ Add Difficulty
Overall Impression	10		☐ Solid Routine ☐ Very Creative ☐ Good Use of Skills	☐ Choppy/Doesn't Flow ☐ Too Much/Jumbled
TOTAL	100		Additional Comments:	
AVERAGE	10.0			

Owner of Central Mississippi Cheer (CMC)
Hometown: Clinton, MS
Squad: Mississippi College
Interesting Fact: As a student at Mississippi College, Hanbery placed in the
top 10 at UCA College Partner Stunt Nationals in 1999 and 2000.

by David Hanbery

"The Art of Choreography"

The term cheeleading brings to mind images of playful and creative ways to encourage a crowd to stand up and make noise. I believe that this is an essential part of our activity, but it doesn't give full justice to the complex art of cheerleading.

Did I shock, surprise, or confuse you by saying "art"? Well let me make a bold comparison. Think about an opera, a Broadway musical, a concerto, or a ballet. They're all arts—performing arts. In the same way, cheerleaders fuse dance, gymnastics, and acrobatics in such a way as to make a distinct, mainstream performing art.

At the heart of each art form is the medium that is used to create a work. In our case, a choreographer is the artist and the cheerleaders are the medium. I believe this is exactly where we choreographers tend to go wrong. In order to create a masterpiece, one must first study the medium, learn to use it properly, and to exploit its strengths while hiding its weaknesses. When a work of art is finished, it's the actual medium that comprises it. In the case of a painting, the colors of paint make up the art; here, the athletes in effect make up the routine.

When I do choreography for a team, I first try to understand the program: the team itself, the individuals, their goals, their attitudes, and their motivations in general. For instance, the kids in my area are not interested in the same things as kids on the West Coast. To give them the same type of routine would be to misuse the talents and abilities of each.

When I walk into a gym, I imagine sculpting the team into a perfect work of art. I want to give them something that represents who they are. This may not be a conventional approach; but it highlights each and every team, and offers something unique to the judges—and, more importantly, to the audiences. On top of this, the athletes get to perform something personal and meaningful to them.

CHAPTER 6

Since cheerleading is a public, performance-based activity, a cheerleader's appearance is constantly up for scrutiny. As a cheerleader, you serve as a role model in your school and a community ambassador; as such, you must pay attention to the way you carry yourself: to what you wear (style), how you handle different situations (attitude), and how you behave toward others (etiquette). It's important to make sure these three elements work together. When they do, you ensure that you and your squad make a positive impression wherever you go. And beyond that, the poise you gain from the experience will help you in situations of all kinds—well into the future.

All eyes on you! Cheerleading is a high-profile activity. Having a clean appearance and a bright disposition are tricks in the cheerleader's trade.

Cheer

Style

▶▶ STYLE

As cheerleading has become more athletic, the standards for style and appearance have evolved. While overdone makeup, an extreme hairstyle, and wacky facial expressions were once staples of a cheer performance, today's standards are more elegant: a bright smile; a clean, natural look; and a simple, elegant pony tail. After all, it's a sport, so its participants want to be taken seriously, and be in the best possible shape—physically and mentally—to execute their complex athletic feats.

When all eyes are on you, it's important to sport a put-together look. A cheerleader's uniform needs to indicate that she is on top of her game! Since cheerleading has developed into a more serious sport, cheer gear has also evolved, and it, too, has become more athletic (not to mention practical).

Gone are the days of overdone hair and caked-on makeup. Simple and elegant is in!

THE LOOK:
The natural look is timeless!

SMILE:
An authentic smile is appealing while on the mat or sidelines.

THE MATERIAL:
With the increased athleticism in today's cheerleading, uniforms are made out of flexible fabrics like Varsity's Motion FLEX®.

DESIGN:
A sharp uniform in bold colors never goes out of style.

THE SHOE:
A cheerleader's shoe needs to be lightweight with a good, supportive sole as well as ankle support.

Changing Times, Changing Gear

Check out how cheerleading trends have evolved over the years and what's driven these changes.

THEN:	NOW:	WHY:
Long, full skirts; usually pleated	Short skirts, either minimally pleated or A-line	Can you imagine doing a stunt in a long skirt? No way! As cheerleading has become more athletic and women's fashion in general has become less conservative, cheerleading skirts have gone from ankle-length to below-the-knee to just-above-the-knee to, now, high-on-the-thigh.
Plain tennis shoes	Reinforced athletic shoes, often in school colors, designed for stunting and tumbling	Advances in shoe technology have allowed cheerleaders to perform more complex, athletic moves. Today's shoes have thick-yet-lightweight soles (to cushion your feet when landing) and stronger ankle support.
Sweaters or T-shirts	Shells, sometimes cropped	A more fitted top is better for stunting, plus looks cleaner and more polished than a looser, airier one. Thanks to synthetic fabrics like Lycra™, you can now cheer more comfortably, too. These fabrics tend to be lighter, provide better ventilation, and allow for freer movement.
Turtleneck sweaters or sweatshirts	Bodysuits or body liners	This item is key when it gets chilly during football season. A thin bodysuit under your shell not only keeps your muscles warm but also looks more polished and uniform. Additionally, most bodysuit fabric is moisture wicking and colorfast.
Plain cotton socks	Enhanced athletic socks	While the overall look of socks hasn't changed that drastically, fabric technology has evolved and socks now keep your feet dry. Often socks are embroidered with your school's mascot or insignia.

TURN THE PAGE TO SEE THE EVOLUTION OF UNIFORMS IN "THE MODERN ERA" OF CHEERLEADING

Uniforms Through the Years

A revolution in uniforms occurred in the 1980s, when cheerleading really started to broaden from leading crowds into the realm of competition. As a cheerleader's duties and activities changed and heightened dramatically, so did the requirements for their uniforms. Freedom of movement now trumped the fashions of the day, so bulky sweaters were replaced by synthetic, more flexible fabrics. The message to uniform manufacturers was to make form meet function.

Over the past twenty years, uniforms have evolved much further in that performance-based direction, because of the continual increase in complexity of the sport's moves, and advances in sports-fabric technology. While polyester once dominated, modern lightweight fabrics that whisk away perspiration and allow for maximum performance capabilities are what's in today. Here's a look at how uniforms and cheer style have changed in more recent times, through the covers of the Varsity Spirit Fashions catalog.

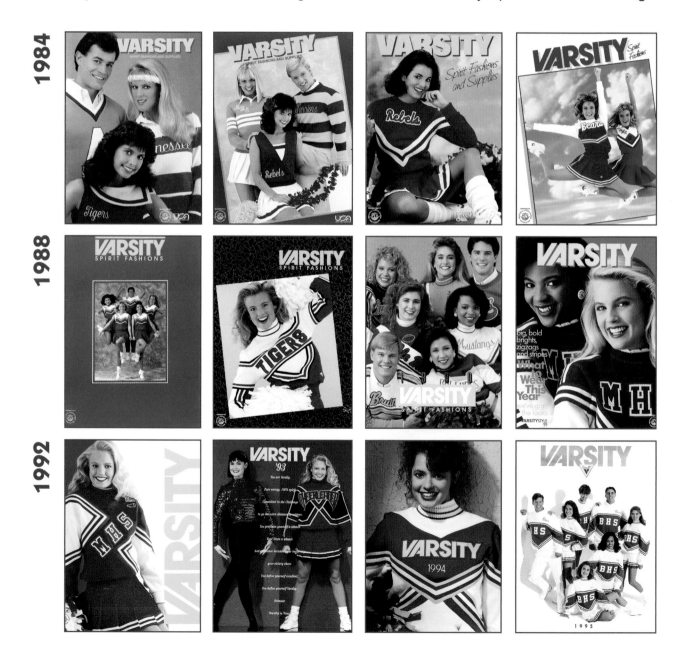

1998

2001

2004

2007

▶▶ Today's Trends

Just as new designer looks are introduced on runways in Milan, Paris, and New York each season, uniform fashions are unveiled each spring with the annual release of uniform catalogs. Some trends are hard to miss, while other less radical adaptations subtly become industry standards. Ultimately, contemporary fashion trends and developments in fabric technology drive these changes. This has resulted in a tremendous variety of options for cheerleading teams today, as new looks continually enter into the fray, and older ones evolve. Just like in mainstream fashion, what's in today may not be in next season—but it can always come back! For example, while midriff tops spiked in popularity for all squads in the late '90s, recently, squads with younger members have moved toward a more conservative look, embracing new top styles that show they have flair without showing as much skin. Cheerleaders can now choose from keyhole, shoulder-baring, or halter styles.

Through all of the changes, one theme has remained the same: cheerleading squads select a look and style that represent the persona of the team and that will deliver a winning look, whether on the football field or the competition mat.

TREND FACTOR

Check out this list of clever ideas:

- Unique fabrics and patterns, featuring holograms, sequins, shattered-glass patterns, and metallic threads
- Appliquéd designs
- Cut-outs along the hemline of the skirt
- Braided trim
- Paw prints or school mascots, often printed or embroidered on the back side of the briefs
- Reverse colors
- Cutie booties
- Custom logos and colors

> Right Look, Right Time

Unlike most sports—where the only outfit choice is between a home and an away uniform—cheerleading's different situations call for a variety of styles and gear. An important part of being a cheerleader is dressing appropriately for the occasion.

Here are the looks you'll want and the times you'll need them:

- **At practice.** Function beats fashion here. Keep things simple: shorts and a sports bra. No makeup.
- **During cheer camp.** Like at practice, you'll want to wear comfortable, functional gear. The days are long, so keep makeup to a minimum.
- **Tryouts.** This is when you're making your first impression. Shoot for a spirited but polished look. Neat-looking workout gear, hair pulled back from face, and no jewelry.
- **In school on game day.** Cheerleaders often wear their uniform to school, but keep your makeup natural and your hairstyle simple.
- **Games and sporting events.** You'll be in your uniform, but you're performing, so you'll want to wear a little makeup.
- **Competitions.** This is where the glitz kicks in! Full makeup, hair pieces, and often some glitter are encouraged.

>> Tasteful vs. Trashy

- A tan from a sunless spray or lotion **vs.** an orange glow from the tanning salon
- An athletic sports bra during practice **vs.** a bra that shows off your décolletage during practice
- A cute mascot sticker or temporary tattoo on your cheek **vs.** heavy makeup and glitter
- A lotion that shimmers, making your gams gleam **vs.** scaly, razor-burned legs
- Touching up in the locker room **vs.** touching up on the sidelines
- Simple stud earrings **vs.** serious bling (chokers, bracelets, dangle earrings, etc.)

Tasteful choices in appearance will highlight your best assets as a cheerleader: strength, gracefulness, and a friendly smile.

Attitude

Any top cheerleader will tell you there's more to getting the right look than the outfit you sport. "Attitude is everything" is a motto that applies to, well, pretty much everything! And in fact, attitude is such a staple to success that there have been *hundreds* of books and articles published about how to achieve a good one. Here's a look at why attitude counts and what it can do for you.

Let Your Attitude Change Your Mind

A fabulous attitude in cheerleading makes you an indispensable asset to your squad. And it saves your sanity! A positive attitude makes more things possible: A problem becomes an *opportunity*, a foe becomes a motivator, an injury becomes a time to rest—and so on. But while your attitude affects everyone around you, how you manage it is up to you.

These University of Alabama partners keep an upbeat attitude and good sense of humor during the long hours of a photo shoot.

Inner Attitude vs. Outer Attitude

Probably you've already realized that attitude is a complex part of your personality. For example, have you ever felt that other people don't see your potential? Or perhaps they think you're amazing when you feel totally lackluster on the inside? Asking yourself questions such as these highlights the difference between inner and outer attitude. First ask yourself, "What's my way of thinking?" Then ask yourself, "What's my way of behaving?" Wow! Attitude is multifaceted, isn't it? That's why it really is everything—it affects you in more ways than you can imagine!

A strong *inner* attitude is crucial to feeling inspired, learning to excel, appreciating your successes, and learning from your failures. An optimistic *outer* attitude encourages your teammates, reflects positively on you, and sets a higher standard for those around you. And attitudes are contagious, so make sure you're infecting people with good vibes, not with foul feelings!

Happiness 101

Inside Cheerleading went to a good-attitude guru to help you handle even the toughest mindset challenges. Tal Ben-Shahar, PhD, teaches positive psychology at Harvard University. With these tips from him, you'll be an attitude ace in no time!

Q: How can someone always be upbeat and positive, no matter what?

A: No person is constantly upbeat and positive. If you try to completely reject your emotions of fear, sadness, or anxiety, it often leads to frustration and unhappiness. Instead, give yourself permission to be human and accept your feelings. Once you do this, you'll actually be much more open to the positive and upbeat emotions you wish to have.

Editor's Insight: So it's kind of like sitting in a hot tub. You give yourself some time to feel the heat, and you get out, and get on with your day, ultimately feeling better!

Q: What are some of the best habits of those who are great leaders and know how to be uplifting to others?

A: Leaders are authentic, they don't try to be someone they're not and aren't all about impressing others. This is easier said than done, but great leaders cultivate a strong sense of self, which then leads others to be themselves too.

Editor's Insight: Aha!

Good leaders are confident but not cocky, and lead by positive example and upbeat attitude.

Q: How can someone handle attitude-killing culprits such as jealousy, boredom, stress, pessimism, etc.?

A: The best way to handle negative emotions is to first acknowledge them so you can deal with them in a healthy way. If we try to ignore feelings, they actually strengthen their hold on us. Recognize the feelings are there, but don't necessarily act on them.

Editor's Insight: So it's like when you refuse to ever talk to your jerky ex-boyfriend again, which in turn makes you think about him even more. By letting yourself acknowledge his presence, you then get over him faster…. hmmm, interesting!

Q: What can an athlete do when he or she is not progressing or is in a slump?

A: Very often, taking time off is what we need. The inclination usually is to work even harder, but sometimes we need to get away from what we're doing to give our mind and body a break.

Editor's Insight: Right, so it's kind of like a tricky puzzle or riddle. You can spend an hour staring at it and getting frustrated, or go take a nap, come back to it, and suddenly "get" it. It's all about being refreshed!

Etiquette

You've set the pace with your fabulous style and polished your attitude, now it's time to showcase yourself. That's where etiquette comes in. This word evokes different feelings in different people. Some think manners. Others think polish. And then there are those who think *blahhh*. Regardless of what you think about etiquette—the esteemed expectations of how to act appropriately—it offers you the opportunity to further prove the honorable role you've embraced by being a cheerleader.

Remember, as a cheerleader, you represent your school and community. And it's important to keep in mind that many of your actions are no longer all about you. As a cheerleader, you've got a responsibility to everyone from your school principal to your teammates to your latest crush, so you want to make sure you show respect for yourself and others.

Etiquette Pointers

GIMME A D-O-N-T! Here are a few unbecoming behaviors you should avoid:

- picking wedgies
- grooming on the sidelines
- cheering only for your favorite player or boyfriend
- incessantly talking to your friends in the stands
- answering your cell phone or text messaging while on the sidelines
- smoking outside during halftime (or, um, ever!)

Open Arms, Not Dirty Looks!

Good etiquette means always welcoming other teams. Typically, a proper welcome includes the basic "welcome cheer" that the home squad performs before the game. The visiting team usually responds by performing its own "introduction cheer," either immediately after or between the first two quarters. Some squads go beyond the basic friendly greeting and actually do something nice for the visiting team, such as offering sports drinks, wall space to hang signs, or the chance to perform a cheer or tumbling pass together.

Sometimes teams and cheerleading squads have rivalries that go beyond friendly competition and are extremely negative. This situation can make it difficult to keep your behavior in check. For example, if rival squad members put trash in your locker room when you visit their school, it's tempting to do the same thing to them when they visit yours. But this kind of behavior is inappropriate and should be discouraged. There's a difference between a rivalry in good fun and nasty rudeness. *Never cross that line.*

Mixing well with members from other teams is part of good cheering sportsmanship.

 ## R-E-S-P-E-C-T!

Proper etiquette includes treating your coaches, other instructors or choreographers, your teammates, and the opposing team and their coaches with maturity and poise. Respect the judgment and decisions of people with authority and/or more experience. If a coach or the captain asks your squad to wear long-sleeved bodysuits for a game or to stop whipping out your cell phones during every break, remember, such requests are typically not up for debate.

It's also important to honor the code of conduct and traditions of your school and squad. If it's customary for cheerleaders to respectfully kneel when a player on either team is injured, then you should do so willingly. These rules were put into place before you came along, and there's probably a good reason why they're still in place. If you have a problem with a rule, aim to handle it with—you got it—respect.

My Story

by Brooklyn Freitag

"My Style"

Style is a personal thing. But competitions can get personal. When it comes to competing, I like to put on a show, work the crowd, and give the audience what they want to see. Competing is my favorite part of cheerleading because I can showcase my style. I love performing and being out there, but I keep in mind that it's not the Brooklyn show. I'm still part of a team, and if each person on the team does his or her absolute best, then it makes the team as a whole amazing.

Like in the fashion world, the styles of cheerleading uniforms change with the times. They used to be made of chunky polyester which was extremely uncomfortable and impractical. Now they're more comfortable and functional, which helps today's cheerleaders do the high-level skills we need to do.

The routines themselves have style as well, and like fashion, they also change with the seasons. I think right now routines are inspired by Broadway shows. We tell stories with the music and with the moves we do during the dance sequences. Routines have become true performances, with many transitions and formations.

Cheerleading styles often reflect the regions they hail from. Various looks, mixed with different talents, make for unique routines. Every year, someone steps up the talent level; and the next year, that talent level is surpassed. This is a healthy

way to push cheerleading forward and to help it grow. Every year the sport progresses and becomes bigger and better. Today we are experiencing a new generation of cheerleading. People enjoy watching the combination of athleticism, grace, energy, and level of skill, all evident in cheerleading as we now know it.

Squad: University of Louisville, Kentucky Elite All Stars
Hometown: Louisville, KY
Interesting Fact: Brooklyn appeared on the cover of the inaugural issue of *Inside Cheerleading* magazine!

CHAPTER 7

World Cups. The Super Bowl. The Olympics. In just about every sport, there's one supreme competition, where top teams come together so athletes and fans around the world can find out who is the best of the best. With the launch of the Cheerleading Worlds in 2004, cheerleaders now have the same chance as other athletes to compete for top honors. The event ushered in a new era in competitive cheerleading and helped to legitimize it among sports fans.

The World Championship title is the crown jewel of All Star cheerleading. In 2006, the Cheer Athletic Wildcats out of Dallas placed first in the large senior coed division.

Who's the Best?

When competitive cheerleading and All Star programs began to take off in the 1980s and 1990s, organized competitions also began to pop up around the country. The UCA and NCA sponsored the first competitions and before long, a number of other local and regional competitions were organized as well. Some of these events expanded into championship-level competitions. The result was that multiple teams, all with high-caliber performances, could claim national championship titles. However, with different teams choosing to attend different competitions, some of the top teams never had the chance to face off. Ultimately, there was no one true competition that awarded titles to the nation's and world's best teams. The debate continued among cheerleaders and fans across the country: Who is truly the best of the best?

Not long after its founding in 2001, the USASF stepped in to settle the score. One of the first issues the USASF addressed was the need for a single definitive competition, one that would bring together the best competitive cheerleading teams from the individual national championship competitions. In 2004 the inaugural Cheerleading Worlds were held in Orlando, Florida. Teams received bids based on their performances at other championship competitions across the country, including the ones sponsored by the Universal Cheerleaders Association, CHEERSPORT, National Cheerleaders Association, American Cheer Power, American Cheerleaders Association and United Spirit Association. Fourteen teams participated in the one-day competition, which was televised nationally by ESPN.

To qualify for the Cheer Worlds, teams must earn bids at qualifying National Championship competitions, such as ones hosted by event organizers Cheerleaders of America (COA), pictured above.

Cheer Athletics' all-girl team wows the crowd with its innovative routine and flawless performance at the first Worlds.

One for the History Books

In that initial outing, only two divisions were contested, all-girl and coed, and only in the most advanced level: level 5. In the all-girl division, Cheer Athletics of Dallas, Texas, one of the first All Star gyms in the country, claimed gold with a jam-packed routine marked by precise execution, attention to detail in form, and intricate stunts that transitioned seamlessly from one to the next. In the coed division, South Florida's Miami Elite dominated with a performance that showcased top-notch tumbling and had some competitors performing passes that stretched the diagonal of the competition mat and back. (See pages 104-105 for a look at this winning routine).

After the inaugural year, the competition grew to include an international division and separate divisions for small teams (between five and twenty members) and large teams (between twenty-one and thirty-five members). The number of competitors also grew from hundreds to thousands. Squads from China, Scotland, and New Zealand have since represented the international cheer community at the Cheerleading Worlds, and as cheerleading grows in popularity, more international teams will surely vie for top honors.

Competition Format

The Cheerleading Worlds consist of two rounds, preliminary and final. Judges include coaches, former cheerleaders, and other experts in the sport. Similar to other competitions, the judging sheet has categories for partner and group stunts, tumbling, basket tosses, pyramids, dance, choreography, and routine composition. Point totals determine which teams earn gold, silver, and bronze medals. At the end of the competition, the winning teams are presented with medals in an elaborate awards ceremony. The gyms also receive a large trophy, commemorating the victory.

It's only fitting that the team that wins the World Championship title takes home a prize commensurate with its grand feat. Teams proudly display these trophies in glass cases at their home gyms. This honor reflects their accomplishment and is a reminder of what it took to achieve glory.

The Premier Sharks strike a pose during their routine at the 2006 Cheer Worlds.

The Memphis Elite coed squad runs through their routine during practice.

Pomp and Circumstance

As well as being a competition, the Cheerleading Worlds provide an opportunity to celebrate the sport. Held as the very last competition of the cheerleading season, it's the final opportunity teams have every year to travel and compete with one another.

A formal banquet on arrival day brings together administrators from each of the different competition companies awarding bids, industry leaders, and coaches of the qualifying teams. The competitors come together the following day for an official opening ceremony event that kicks off the competition itself. The ceremony is led by the president of the USASF and reinforces the spirit of friendly competition. Squads gather to greet each other before taking to the mat to face off. Sometimes exhibition performances are a part of the opening ceremony.

Most teams stay in nearby in hotel complexes close to Orlando's competition arena. This setup gives the area the feel of a temporary "athletes' village," like at the Olympics. It also allows teams from all over the world to get to know one another.

The competition itself consists of two rounds spread over two days. Teams with the strongest performances during the season receive an automatic invitation to the final round of competition, while others advance to finals based upon their performance in the preliminary round. Teams that advance from the preliminary round are announced publicly in the arena and, the following day, face off against the teams who have already qualified for finals.

During the competition, a trade show for industry suppliers is also held. Each vendor has a booth in which to present its products to coaches, competitors, and other industry members. The festive atmosphere includes product demonstrations, raffles, give-away promotions, seminars, and speaking engagements by leaders in the industry.

After the competition is over and the awards have been handed out, a closing ceremony marks the official end. Finally, a dance party is held, giving all participants the opportunity to come together and let loose before the new season begins!

Left: Arlington's Spirit of Texas squad celebrates a routine well done. The team was rewarded for its stellar performance by placing second at the 2004 World Championships.

2005
GOLD
CHAMPION
THE CHEERLEADING WORLDS
USA

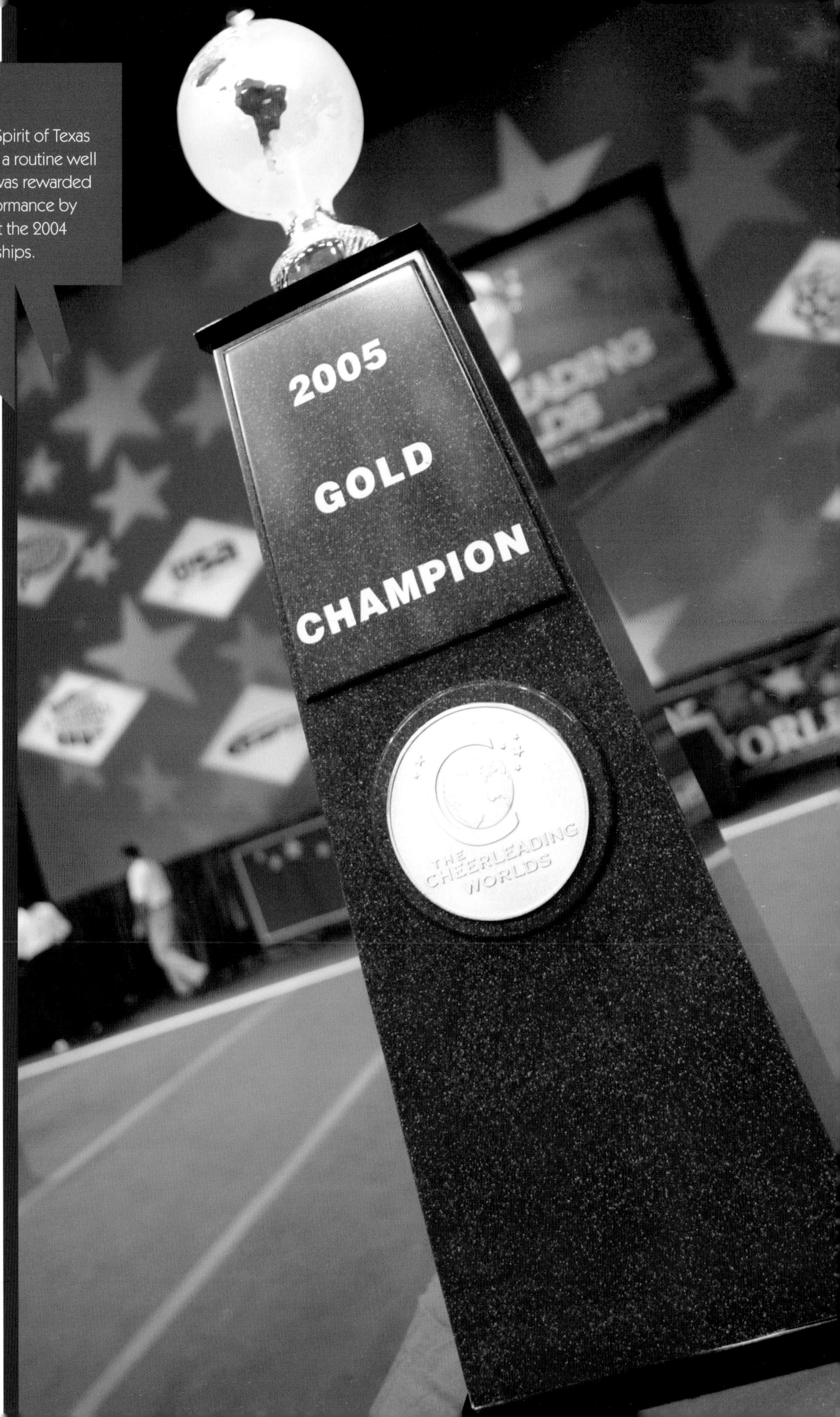

⏩ The Right Stuff

To win a World Championship title, a team must perform an intricate routine with a flawless combination of stunts, tumbling, baskets, pyramids, dance, and transitions. Here's a look at Miami Elite's winning routine from the inaugural Cheerleading Worlds. This routine had that perfect combination and flow to earn gold in the coed division.

⏩ Routine opens with nine standing fulls, followed by four front handsprings, front tucks, and seven back handsprings to double fulls

⏩ Multiple kick double baskets followed by a kick-kick double basket in the center and squad standing back tucks

⏩ Dance sequence: up front with six ball-up heel stretches to arabesque double-down

⏩ Tumbling segment: seventeen double fulls, plus front tumbling and combination tumbling (including fronts and Arabian throughs, and a whip immediate double)

⏩ Inverted pyramid to heel-stretch pyramid with another dance sequence as well as stunt combinations

⏩ All groups come together to wolf wall

⏩ Jump segment: pike jump to toe touch to front hurdlers

⏩ Eight-count of dance (guys and girls) to closing pose

Miami Elite embodies perfection at the 2004 World Championships of All Star Cheerleading. The team delivered an amazing routine packed with advanced skills like this stretch pyramid with two Arabian throughs to doubles in front of a pyramid **(front)** and a kick double basket sequence **(far left)**.

In the History Books

There will only be one set of inaugural Cheerleading Worlds medalists! Here are the teams that made that mark.

ALL GIRL

COED

CHEER ATHLETICS - GOLD 455.5

MIAMI ELITE - GOLD 452.0

MARYLAND TWISTERS F5 - SILVER 419.0

SPIRIT OF TEXAS - SILVER 447.5

AMERICAN CHEER - BRONZE 409.0

MEMPHIS ELITE - BRONZE 437.5

My Story

by Cassondra Machac

"I am a World Champion"

I came to Cheer Athletics in seventh grade, and since then, it's become a second home to me. I was a Level-10 gymnast, and a friend invited me to her practice at Cheer Athletics. That was all I needed to see. The coaches and all the girls were great and everyone was very tolerant of my funny-looking gymnastics-style jumps. My first year I was on the "Jags," a large, very competitive junior-level team. I didn't even pay that much attention to the competitions— I was just having a great time! I remember telling my mom that everyone was getting quite excited about this NCA competition coming up, but I had no idea why. It wasn't long before I found out, though. The Jags always dominated there—we once won seven NCA titles in a row! Every year we went to NCA, we were trying to break the record we'd set there the year before. It was a great challenge, but we did keep breaking records the entire time I was on the team!

The first Cheerleading Worlds were held during my third year with Cheer Athletics. I was one of the youngest girls to be asked to be on the Supercats (the senior all-girl team). We had an amazing competition overall and went on to become the first-ever World Champions in the sport of competitive cheerleading. It was amazing just to be there, but winning was a moment I will never forget! Thanks to my wonderful coaches and teammates, I am now part of cheerleading history!

Squad: Cheer Athletics
Hometown: Plano, Texas
Interesting Fact: As a competitive gymnast, Cassondra trained at World Olympic Gymnastics Academy, the same gym as 2004 Olympic Champion Carly Patterson.

CHAPTER 8

As a cheerleader, you have your poms, your megaphone, and your signs, but there's something else—or someone else—that can be a great ally in firing up your crowd. Is it a bird? Is it a plane? No! It's your school mascot buzzing all over the arena, bringing people in the crowd to their feet and generating roaring applause from the stands! Most schools have mascots on their spirit teams because of the integral role they play in leading the crowd.

Let's take a stroll back through the early days of mascots, find out what it takes to become one, learn about camps and career opportunities, and then check out their costumes! Who knows—after finding out more, you may decide you want to step into the role yourself one day!

Larger than life, the University of Tennessee's mascot, Smokey, leads the spirit pack and helps bring roaring fans to their feet.

Don't Forget

the Mascots!

▶▶ A Brief History of Mascots

When schools started to use mascots, they often adopted animals for them—literally. In the nineteenth century schools actually kept living, breathing creatures in cages on or near campus and would put them on display at athletic events. Concern for the animals' safety—and sometimes the students' safety as well—eventually brought the practice into question. A few schools remedied the situation by creating safer conditions for their animals. Baylor University, for example, still keeps live bears on campus. These animals are cared for by specialists who also provide educational programs about the bears to the local community. Other schools donated their real animals to zoos and came up with alternatives for games.

Hanging on to tradition, the University of Tennessee has the best of both worlds, mascot in body and costume.

When schools abandoned the idea of live mascots, spirited students took matters into their own hands. Frederick Fox, a student in Princeton University's class of 1939, borrowed a tiger skin his father was rumored to have won in a card game and began wearing it to football games. Since the Princeton team's quick moves and orange-and-black socks had already prompted sportscasters to compare them to a striped beast, the connection was logical, and the tiger, already a Princeton symbol, became the official mascot. Other schools followed "suit" by introducing costumed characters to their crowds. University of California, Berkeley's Oski the Bear was introduced in 1941, Ohio University's Bobcat in 1960, and Brown University's Bruno the Bear in the 1960s.

As student mascots became popular features at football games, other sports teams caught on and the mascot's responsibilities grew. Some schools maintain multiple costumes, with a crew of students willing to don them. For example Brown University owns two costumes and selects five students each year who divvy up a list of events the mascot is required to attend. Often seasoned mascots (usually graduating seniors) train newer mascots and determine who will earn the title of lead mascot the following year.

The love for a mascot is not always constant. In fact, some schools have changed their mascots through the years, for a multitude of reasons. The University of West Georgia cheered for five different mascots—the Aggie, the Hillbilly, the Bull

Pup, the Goat, and the Brave—before adopting the Wolf in 2006. For years the Grand Rapids Community College's Raider wore Civil War Union blues, but he was mistaken for so many other characters (everything from a Keystone cop to a scrubbing bubble), the school updated his uniform a few years ago to give him more of an "Indiana Jones" look.

In the '70s mascots named for Native Americans drew many complaints, especially ones shown in less-than-noble lights. And recently, groups such as the National Coalition on Racism in Sports and Media officially asked sports teams to stop disparaging Native Americans. Soon after, the National Collegiate Athletic Association (NCAA) prevented nineteen schools from hosting NCAA events until their Native American mascots were changed.

Political correctness has not been the only reason behind mascot reform. Over the years audiences have taken offense at other mascot names and/or symbols for other reasons. Some religious groups, for instance, recently targeted the Arizona State University Sun Devils, with their devil mascot, as drawing too many people into "devil worshipping."

In some cases it has been the student body that has initiated a change of mascot. In 1986 students at the University of California, Santa Cruz raised money to hold a referendum to change the school's mascot to the banana slug—a peaceful, native species that they felt represented their population. The banana slug was favored fifteen to one over the administration's preferred sea lion, and the change was made.

Hardest-Working Animal in the Cheer Business

Some of a mascot's work is obvious on game day, but there's an inside to every story—or in this case, what goes on underneath that costume! In addition to dancing, playing, participating in stunts, performing skits, instigating pranks, signing autographs, doing push-ups when their team scores, and staying through the game—even when the crowd leaves early— mascots often face heat, exhaustion, and rashes from too much time spent inside a sweltering costume. They also risk attacks from mobs of rival teams' students who want to hurt their rival's mascot or steal its mask as a trophy. Needless to say, this is rarely the description posted on advertisements for mascot tryouts!

This Ram still manages to groove, despite his oversized head and heavy costume.

⏵ TOP-NOTCH MASCOTS NEED:

An Interest in Sports.

Most mascot events are sports oriented, and it helps to understand the rules so you know when to clap, get excited, or feign outrage.

Endurance.

Games can be long and hot when you're wearing a twenty- to forty-pound costume.

Groovy Moves.

The band can start playing at any time, and you're the dancer in the spotlight!

A Few Good Stunts.

While you won't be expected to top a pyramid or fly in a basket toss in most costumes—it wouldn't be safe—if you show your crowd a few basic stunts, they'll shower you with praise.

Sense of Humor.

One look in the mirror, and you'll know why this is important.

Tryouts

People from a variety of backgrounds—gymnastics, dance, theater and even child psychology—are attracted to becoming mascots. But many mascots have no applicable background at all, unless you count dressing up for Halloween. A few are cheerleaders looking for a change. Some squads offer mascot duties to someone who does not make the cheer squad during tryouts. Others reserve the costume for a cheerleader who can't stunt due to an injury.

▷ TRYOUT TIPS: FOR THE SQUAD

1 **Determine what you need from your mascot.** How important are dance moves, stunts, strength, and a sense of humor? Clearly describe to the candidates what you are looking for, and score tryouts accordingly.

2 **Be sure that at the tryout, the judges don't know who's in the costume.** Keeping tryouts anonymous helps keep scores fair and allows judges to focus on the mascot the crowd will see, not the person inside the costume.

3 **Advertise! Advertise! Advertise!** The more you hype the mascot tryouts, the more likely you are to attract talented newcomers. Old-timers can take a new mascot underwing (or under paw or hoof!), and delegate who will do what during the sport season.

You can never tell what kind of person is hiding behind the mask!

TRYOUT TIPS: FOR THE MASCOT

 Get a feel for the costume ahead of time. Borrow one, try it on, and walk around so you can practice "mascot moves" before tryout day.

2 **Watch the current mascot.** Decide whether to be similar or totally different. Do the school and cheer squad want a new mascot personality or should you stick with what you see?

3 **Review the team's list of expectations.** They should list what they would like to see at the tryout and give you a clear sense of what they will expect from the mascot during the season. If a score sheet is available, study it!

 Lights, cameras, action! Practice (in costume if possible) and videotape your routine so you can critique and improve it before the actual tryout day.

Mascot tryouts can be as rigorous as cheerleading tryouts—the more visible the mascot, the more people will vie for the opportunity to become one. In rare situations, schools maintain total secrecy by having their tryouts judged by outgoing former mascots—even the cheerleaders aren't involved. These schools are serious about maintaining the mascot mystique!

At a few schools, mascot tryouts are an annual affair where students, sans costume, conduct pranks around campus. The student who attracts the most attention with an original and daring prank or several pranks in a row—hopefully without getting caught by campus security—secures the mascot suit.

Ideal mascot candidates are able to:

 Fit in the costume.

Express themselves through body language.

Be comfortable around people—children, alumni, and students.

Find the humor in everyday events, but know when it's time to be serious.

Protect themselves from hordes of rioting sore losers.

Commit time to sporting events, public appearances, and cheer practices.

Great Expectations

Cheerleaders who have their hearts set on a mascot that can bounce off a mini-trampoline through a flaming hoop while grabbing a thrown basketball and dunking it into a regulation net need to stop watching so many movies! Here are some basic questions to keep in mind.

The University of Kentucky's Wildcat mascot is known for its dancing abilities. Tryouts to become the Wildcat focus on how applicants interact with the fans and lead a crowd but also how well the person dances.

Freestyle Dance. Can your mascot groove to the latest songs with a variety of moves?

School Fight Song Dance. How will the mascot be able to pep up the crowd when the school fight song is played?

Prop Skills. How does the mascot handle props such as poms and batons? Can he or she use the prop in one way then quickly switch to using it in another way (for example, conducting the band with the baton, then turning around and balancing that same baton on his nose)?

Skits. Give each mascot one minute to act out an original skit. Is there a punch line? Is the skit relevant to a specific sport, a rival team, or your own team? How would a crowd react if this skit was performed at halftime? Is it clean enough for kids?

Body Language. Call out an emotion or situation and have the mascot react. How well does the mascot express anger, fear, concern, respect, and cheer—without a voice?

Endurance. If the entire spirit squad performs as many push-ups as points on the scoreboard, then the mascot needs to prove that he or she can do the same. Ask the mascot to drop and give you fifty!

The One-Minute-It's-All-Yours Drill. Ask the mascot to show you any additional talents he or she may have. Perhaps one mascot can juggle, another ride a unicycle, a third Rollerblade in costume, and a fourth perform a magic trick. Who would have known? That's why you ask.

Entrance and Exit. How did the mascot enter and exit the room? Did his or her entrance/exit grab and hold your attention? Was it spirited, funny, surprising, or original?

▷▷ Camp in Costume

When the squad heads to cheerleading camp, the mascot does not just tag along for fun. While mascots generally go to camp with their cheer squads, once there, they train separately. Camp for mascots is a real circus—with dancing bears, prankster clowns, and lions jumping through hoops (or at least attempting to)! As a mascot at camp, your time will be spent improving your current technique, learning new moves, building stunts, and dancing—just as the cheerleaders are doing. But while the cheerleaders are sweating outside in the sun, most of your activities will take place in air-conditioned bliss—which you'll be grateful for, since you will spend a lot of camp time in costume.

At camp, mascots often develop "mini-skits" to bring back to campus for the upcoming season. Together, the mascots brainstorm common situations that arise

and how to react to them in a crowd-pleasing way. For example, when a fan poses with the mascot for a photo, it's more fun for everyone if the mascot does something unusual—picks up the person, leans heavily on his shoulder, or plants a big smooch on her unsuspecting lips. At camp, mascots work to come up with such responses and to practice the timing of them and any necessary motions involved. The goal is to create a mini-skit that is perfectly executed but totally natural and unrehearsed in feeling.

The wildest animals will take advantage of the camp's downtime as well, showing up for meals and social activities in full costume. Providing an unexpected or impromptu show will entertain a group that doesn't often get to be the ones entertained—the cheerleaders!

Mascot camps yield animals and outlaws of all shapes and sizes! Camp time helps mascots master new moves and improve overall technique.

▷ A Career in Costume?

Since a mascot's image stays with the team season after season, it often becomes the team's most identifiable icon. Players and children are more likely to request toys, sports equipment, or souvenirs branded with the mascot's likeness than with that of a mere mortal. And though few mascots end up in costume full-time after college graduation, there are opportunities at the professional sports level, in theme parks, and in certain advertising campaigns.

For those mascots who do make it to the big leagues, the pay can be enormous—but so can the expectations. While mascots in the National Basketball Association made an average of $150,000 for a six-month season in 2002, they earned their keep: each was expected to participate in hundreds of publicity stops, promoting both the team and its merchandise. In one year, the Houston Rockets's mascot, Clutch the Bear, made three hundred promotional appearances. Other professional mascots are not as well paid, with some earning as little as $150 per game.

Knock It Up a Notch

Mascots seeking to improve school spirit should consider how the school is seen by others. To do this, look no further than your school's public relations department. Many colleges and universities have an entire staff of people dedicated to promoting their school's image. High schools, even if they don't have an official PR person, will have teachers who advise the school yearbook, newspaper, and athletics groups. Ask a PR professional or appropriate teacher what the mascot could do to help boost spirit. Or better yet, brainstorm with the cheer squad and leave a copy of your ideas with that person.

If traditionally your school mascot only cheers for one specific team, consider broadening your role by cheering for some of your school's other teams. If that is too much of a time commitment, adopt an extra body to fill the costume! As mentioned previously, some schools have teams of five or more students who share more than one costume. This way, the mascot is able to appear at more events. Even one more person and one more costume would mean you can double the number of events the mascot attends.

Can't find that extra mascot? Chances are your school doesn't hold tryouts. Talk with the cheer squad about strengthening the spirit program by starting mascot tryouts. This is the best way to attract an extra mascot and to add that extra boost to your spirit program.

And remember—sometimes simple steps take enormous effort, so use your mascot prowess and patience to gently push for your cause to be heard!

> FORBIDDEN Activities

Things mascots should NEVER do:

- Talk in costume
- Scare small children
- Do anything you'd be embarrassed to see on the front page of a newspaper
- Remove the mask in public

Shhhh, don't tell anyone who's in here!

My Story
"A Day in the Life of a Mascot"

On the prowl from dusk 'til dawn, my work is seemingly never done! Here's a look at a day in the life of the Princeton mascot.

6:00 a.m. Wake up and hit the showers. Why so early? So nobody sees if the Tiger uses the girls' bathroom or the boys' bathroom!

7:00 a.m. Breakfast! Frosted Flakes (of course!), milk, and a banana. Hang out with the five other people who wake up this early for breakfast on a Saturday morning.

8:00 a.m. Clean milk off whiskers. Review calculus homework assignment. Catnap.

9:00 a.m Join the Princeton University Band as they march around the campus, waking up all the students—and anyone within a mile radius—to remind them it's game day!

10:00 a.m. Last stop on the band's parade—the Princeton University Store. Check out new merchandise. Browse the book section and autograph customers' books on the university. Pay my U-Store bill!

11:30 a.m. Randomly select a school cafeteria and show my student ID to get in. (It reads "The" Princeton Tiger.) Skip the hot foods—too messy for the costume and too heavy for game day. Grab a stack of bread and make sandwiches from the salad bar. (This tiger's a vegetarian.) Add four pieces of fruit and a bowl of ice cream to my tray. Fill my oversize water bottle. Join a table of unsuspecting students. Eat the ice cream. Convince the students to help me wrap the sandwiches and fruit in napkins and hide them in my costume so I can sneak them out of the cafeteria undetected.

12:00 p.m. Exit cafeteria. Wave good-bye to cafeteria staff very carefully—I do not want the apples up my sleeve to roll down to my boots.

12:20 p.m. Arrive at football stadium. Join Princeton cheerleaders, who have been warming up since 11:30. Distribute sandwiches and fruit to hungry cheerleaders who missed lunch.

12:30 p.m. Hear the band nearby. Find them playing for tailgate parties in the parking lot. Dance with alumni. Play with kids. Follow band into stadium. Get stopped by stadium guards for looking suspicious. Convince them I'm just a big old pussycat. Enter stadium.

1:00 p.m. Kick off. Watch football team beat up on Harvard. Wonder why Harvard doesn't have a mascot. Feel sorry for Harvard students.

1:10 p.m. Play with kids. Sign autographs. Sit with students and let them guess whether they know me. Give vague hints but leave them guessing.

1:30 p.m. Join the band as they prepare outside the end zone for another fabulous halftime show. Play Frisbee with a spare hat. Offer to hold the announcer's trumpet during the show. March onto the field at halftime playing the announcer's trumpet. Dance with a band member then drag a cheerleader onto the field to be my dance partner.

1:50 p.m. Walk through the stands. Play with kids. Wonder why people wearing Harvard sweatshirts are sitting in the Princeton section.

1:55 p.m. Realize I'm on the wrong side of the stadium. Hightail it to the Princeton side before anything unruly happens.

2:00 p.m. Visit the band. Rub my tummy. Let them feed me chocolate.

2:10 p.m. Make sure I've visited every kid I can find. Autograph programs.

2:45 p.m. Join cheerleaders as crowd sings "Old Nassau" at the end of the game. March with band for post-game parade. Notice the nine kids who are following me and wonder why their parents seem totally fine with this.

3:00 p.m. Parade ends at Woodrow Wilson Fountain. Remind myself cats don't like water. Watch the band bunny-hop into the fountain. Realize I'm still in a marching line. Realize the kids have joined me in line. Really wonder why the parents don't seem to mind. Forget to step out of line. Jump into fountain. Be glad it's only waist deep. Dance with the kids in the fountain. Wonder how much babysitting would pay.

3:30 p.m. Drag my soaked-to-the-skin self back to the dorm. Jump in the shower to clean off any fountain chlorine. Accidentally frighten someone who comes in to go to the bathroom.

4:00 p.m. Catnap number two.

4:30 p.m. Read three chapters for Russian literature course. Draw graphs for macroeconomics course. Ask roommate to explain molecular biology lab assignment for next week.

6:00 p.m. Dinner at favorite campus cafeteria.

7:00 p.m. Discuss evening plans with friends. Decide whether to go watch the student production of *Cat on a Hot Tin Roof* or go dancing. Pick dancing. I'm such a party animal!

The highest standards in Safety, Education, Sportsmanship

Airborne/Aerial: To be free of contact with a person or the performing surface.

Airborne Tumbling Skill: An aerial maneuver involving hip-over-head rotation in which a person uses his or her body and the performing surface to propel himself/herself away from the performing surface.

Assisted-Flipping Mount: An entrance skill into a stunt in which a top person performs a hip-over-head rotation while in direct physical contact with a base or top person when passing through the inverted position. (See "Braced Flip," "Suspended Flip/Roll.")

Assisted Tumbling: Any form of physical assistance to an individual performing a tumbling skill. This does not apply to gymnastic oriented "stunts" permitted at each level.

Awesome: See "Cupie."

Back Spot: The person in the back of a stunt mainly responsible for protecting the head and shoulder area of a top person.

Back Walkover: A non-aerial tumbling skill where one moves backward into an arched position, with the hands making contact with the ground first, then rotates the hips over the head and lands on one foot/leg at a time.

Backward Roll: A non-aerial tumbling skill where one rotates backward into or through an inverted position by lifting the hips over the head and shoulders while curving the spine to create a motion similar to a ball "rolling" across the floor.

Barrel Roll: See "Log Roll."

Base: A person who is in direct weight-bearing contact with the performance surface and provides support for another person. The person(s) who holds, lifts, or tosses a top person into a stunt. (See also "New Base(s)" and "Original Base(s).")

Basket Toss: A toss with no more than four bases, two of which use their hands to interlock wrists.

Block: A gymnastic term referring to the increase in height created by using one's hand(s) and upper body power to push off the performing surface during a tumbling skill. The momentary airborne position created by blocking is legal for all levels.

Block Cartwheel: A momentarily airborne cartwheel created by the tumbler blocking through the shoulders against the performing surface during the execution of the skill.

Brace: A physical connection that helps to provide stability to a top person.

Braced Flip: A stunt in which a top person performs a hip-over-head rotation while in constant physical contact with another top person(s).

Cartwheel: A non-aerial gymnastic skill where one supports the weight of the body with the arm(s) while rotating sideways through an inverted position landing on one foot at a time.

Catcher: One of the person(s) responsible for the safe landing of a top person during a stunt.

Connected Tumbling: Physical contact between two or more individuals performing tumbling skills simultaneously.

BRACE

CATCHER

BASKET TOSS

U. S. ALL STAR
USASF
FEDERATION
FOR CHEER & DANCE TEAMS
The highest standards in Safety, Education, Sportsmanship

Cradle: A release move in which catchers, with palms up, catch the top person by placing one arm under the back and the other under the thighs of the top person. The top person must land face up in a pike position.

Cupie: An extended stunt where a top person has both feet together in the hand(s) of the base(s). Also referred to as an "Awesome."

Dirty Bird (D-Bird): Toss to a laid out X-position to the back of the base, through the base's legs and typically transitioning to a scooper.

Dismount: The movement from a stunt or pyramid to a cradle or the performing surface. The movement from a cradle to the performing surface is not considered to be a dismount.

Dive Roll: An aerial forward roll where the hands and feet are off of the performing surface simultaneously.

Double-Leg Stunt: See "Stunt."

Downward Inversion: A stunt or pyramid in which an inverted top person's center of gravity is moving toward the performing surface.

Downward Motion: The movement of one's center of gravity toward the performing surface.

Drop: Dropping to the knee, thigh, seat, front, back, or split position onto the performing surface from an airborne position or inverted position without first bearing most of the weight on the hands/feet which breaks the impact of the drop.

Eighteen Inches Above Extended Arm Level: The maximum distance allowed between the highest points of a base's extended arm and the lowest point of a top person's body during a release move in Level 5 only.

Entrance Skill: The beginning or mounting phase of a tumbling skill or stunt.

Extended Arm Level: The distance from the performing surface to the highest point of a base's arm(s) when standing upright with the arm(s) fully extended over the head. Extended arms do not necessarily define an "extended stunt." See "Extended Stunt" for further clarification.

Extended Position: A top person supported by a base(s) with fully extended arms. Extended arms do not necessarily define an "extended stunt." See "Extended Stunt" for further clarification.

Extended Single-Leg Stunt: An extended stunt where the top person has primary weight on one leg.

Extended Stunt: When the entire body of the top person is extended in an upright position over the base(s). (Examples of stunts that are not considered "extended stunts": Chairs, torches, flat backs, arm-n-arms, and straddle lifts. These are stunts where the bases' arms are extended overhead, but are *not* considered to be "extended stunts" since the height of the body of the top person is similar to a shoulder/prep level stunt.)

Extension Prep, or Prep, or Half: When the top person is being held at shoulder level by the base(s).

Flat Back: A stunt in which the top person is lying horizontally and is usually supported by two or more bases.

Flip: An aerial skill that involves hip-over-head rotation without contact with the performing surface as the body passes through the inverted position.

THE WORLD CHAMPIONSHIP OF ALL STAR CHEE

2006

CUPIE

Flipping Toss: A toss where the top person rotates through an inverted position.

Flyer: The person(s) on top of a stunt or toss. Also referred to as the "Top Person" or "Partner."

Forward Roll: A non-aerial tumbling skill where one rotates forward through an inverted position by lifting the hips over the head and shoulders while curving the spine to create a motion similar to a ball "rolling" across the floor.

Free-Flipping Mount: Immediately prior to the stunt, the entry into a stunt where the top person passes through an inverted position without physical contact with a base, brace, or the performing surface.

Front Limber: A non-aerial tumbling skill where one rotates forward through an inverted position to a non-inverted position by arching the legs and hips over the head and down to the performing surface landing on both feet/legs at the same time.

Front Spot: A person positioned in front of a stunt who may also add additional support or height to that stunt. (Also known as "fourth base.")

Front Tuck: A tumbling skill in which the tumbler generates momentum upward to perform a forward flip. (Also known as "punch front.")

Front Walkover: A non-aerial tumbling skill where one rotates forward through an inverted position to a non-inverted position by arching the legs and hips over the head and down to the performing surface landing one foot/leg at a time.

Full: A 360-degree twisting rotation.

Full-Up Toe Touch: A non-flipping skill (typically performed in a dismount or toss) in which one performs a 360-degree turn before executing a toe touch.

Ground Level: To be at the height of or supported by the performing surface.

Half: See "Extension Prep."

Hand/Arm Connection: The physical contact between two or more individuals using the hand(s)/arm(s).

Handspring: Springing off the hands by putting the weight on the arms and using a strong push from the shoulders; can be done either forward or backward.

Handstand: A straight body inverted position where the arms are extended straight by the head and ears.

Hanging Pyramid: A pyramid in which one or more persons are suspended off the performing surface by one or more top persons. Hanging pyramids must remain upright.

Helicopter Toss: A stunt where a top person in a horizontal position is tossed to rotate around a vertical axis (like helicopter blades) before being caught by original bases.

Inversion: See "Inverted"; it is the act of being inverted.

Inverted: When the top person's shoulders are below her/his waist and at least one foot is above her/his waist. Arch-back dismounts to a cradle are not considered inverted.

Jump: An airborne position not involving hip-over-head rotation created by using one's own feet and lower body power to push off the performance surface.

FLYER

GROUND LEVEL

INVERTED

HAND/ARM
CONNECTION

The highest standards in Safety, Education, Sportsmanship

Kick Arch: Type of trick that involves the straight ride to a kick with one leg and an arch out of the trick into the cradle position.

Kick Full: Skill, typically in a toss, that involves a kick and a 360-degree twisting rotation. A one-quarter turn performed by the top person during the kick portion is customary and permitted to initiate the twist.

Knee (Body) Drop: Dropping to the knees, seat, thigh, or splits from an airborne position without first bearing the majority of the weight on the hands or feet.

Layout: A stretched body position, straight, hollow, or slightly arched.

Layout Step Out: A layout where the tumbler scissors his or her legs and lands with one foot in front of the other.

Leap Frog: A braced top person is transitioned from one set of bases to another or back to the original bases by going through the arms of the brace. The top person remains upright and stays in continuous contact with the brace while transitioning.

Log Roll: A release move whereby the top person's body rotates at least 360 degrees while remaining parallel to the performing surface. (Also known as "barrel roll.")

Mount: See "Stunt."

Multi-based Stunt: A stunt having two or more bases not including the back spot.

New Base(s): Bases previously not in direct contact with the top person of a stunt.

Non-Inverted Position: The body is upright. The top person's shoulders are at or above the waist.

One-half-Twist Toe Touch: A non-flipping skill in which one performs a 180-degree twist before executing a toe touch.

Onodi: Starting from a back-handspring position after pushing off, the tumbler performs a half twist to the hands, ending the skill as a front-handspring step out.

Original Base(s): A base which is in contact with the top person during the initiation of the stunt.

Paper Dolls: Identical single-leg stunts executed by top people bracing each other while in the single leg position. The stunts may or may not be extended.

Partner: See "Flyer."

Pike: Body bent forward at the hips while the legs are kept straight.

Prep: See "Extension Prep."

Prep-Level: When the height of the bases' hands and at least one foot of the top person are at shoulder-level (also known as shoulder-height). Chairs, torches, flatbacks, arm-n-arms, and straddle lifts are considered prep-level stunts.

Primary Support: Supporting a majority of the weight of the top person.

Prone Position: A face down, flat body position.

Prop: An object that can be manipulated.

Punch: See "Rebound."

Pyramid: A grouping of multiple stunts that may or may not be connected to create a visual effect. Individuals standing at ground level may be incorporated into the grouping.

LAYOUT

PYRAMID

LAYOUT STEP OUT

PIKE

Rebound: A gymnastic term referring to an airborne position not involving hip-over-head rotation created by using one's own feet and lower body power to bounce off the performance surface from a tumbling skill. Also known as "Punch."

Release Move: When the base(s) and top person become free of contact with each other and the top person comes back to the original set of bases. A single base toss to a stunt from the ground is neither considered a release move nor a toss. This interpretation applies to stunts only, not pyramids.

Reload: Returning to the loading position with both feet of the top person in the hands of the bases.

Retake: Reloading to a stunt, whereby the top person brings one foot to the ground prior to reloading.

Rewind: A free-flipping release move used as an entrance skill into a stunt.

Round Off: The tumbler, with a push off on one leg, plants hand(s) on floor while swinging the legs upward in a fast cartwheel motion. The feet snap down together and land at the same time on the performing surface.

Running Tumbling: Tumbling that is performed with a running start and/or involves a punch, cartwheel, round off, round-off handspring, etc., used to gain momentum as an entry to another skill. Any type of forward momentum/movement prior to execution of the tumbling skill(s) is defined as "running tumbling."

Scooper: An entrance/transition skill into a stunt in which a person (usually a top person) passes between the legs and under the torso of another person (usually a base).

Scrunch Toss: See "Sponge Toss."

Second Level: Any person being supported away from the performing surface by one or more bases.

Second-Level Leap Frog: Same as leap frog but performed at any level above ground level.

Series Front and/or Back Handsprings: Multiple front and/or back handsprings performed consecutively by an individual.

Show and Go: A transitional stunt where a stunt passes through an extended level and lands into a loading position or non-extended stunt.

Shoulder-Stand Level: A stunt in which the top person's hips are at the same height they would be if in a shoulder stand.

Shushunova: A straddle jump (toe touch) landing in a prone support.

Single-Based Double Awesome or Cupie: A single base supporting two top persons who have both feet in each hand of the base; see definition of "Awesome" or "Cupie."

Single-Based Split Catch: A single base extending a top person (who is in an upright position having knees forward) by holding both inner thighs as the top person typically performs a high "V" motion, creating an "X" with the body. This is an illegal stunt.

Single-Based Stunt: A stunt using a single base for support.

Single-Leg Stunt: See "Stunt."

Sponge Toss: A stunt with multiple bases, which have their hands gripping the top person's feet prior to the toss.

Spotted Tumbling: See "Assisted Tumbling."

SHOW AND GO

USASF
U. S. ALL STAR FEDERATION
FOR CHEER & DANCE TEAMS
The highest standards in Safety, Education, Sportsmanship

Spotter: A person whose primary responsibility is the protection of another during the performance of a skill. Spotters must be in direct contact with the performing surface, and be attentive to the skill being spotted. A "Back Spotter" is required for each extended stunt. (See also "Back Spot.") Spotters must be in the proper position to prevent injuries, but they do not have to be in direct contact with the stunt. A spotter cannot stand so that his or her torso is under a stunt. They cannot have both hands directly supporting under the sole of the top person's foot/feet. A spotter may grab the wrist(s) of the base(s), other parts of the base(s) arms, or the top person's legs (ankles), but he or she does not have to touch the stunt at all. All spotters must be team members and be trained in proper spotting techniques. Spotters may also be counted as a base in some cases (e.g. transitional stunts).

Squishy (Toss): See "Sponge Toss."

Standing Tumbling: A tumbling skill (or series of skills) performed from a standing position without any previous forward momentum. Any number of steps backward prior to execution of tumbling skill(s) is defined as "standing tumbling."

Straight Cradle: A release move from a stunt to a catching position where no skill (i.e. turn, kick, twist, etc.) is performed.

Straight Ride: The body position of a top person performing a toss that doesn't involve any trick in the air. It is a straight line position that teaches the top to reach and to obtain maximum height on toss.

Stunt: Any skill in which a top person is supported above the performance surface by one or more persons. Also referred to as a "mount." A stunt is determined to be "Single" or "Double" leg by the number of legs that the top person has being primarily supported by a base(s).

Suspended Flip/Roll: A stunt in which a top person performs a hip-over-head rotation while in constant physical contact with a person(s) who is in direct weight-bearing contact with the performing surface.

Tension Roll or Drop: A pyramid or stunt in which the base(s) and top(s) lean in formation until the top person(s) leaves the base(s) without assistance.

Three-Quarter Front Flip: A forward hip-over-head rotation from an upright position to a cradle position.

Tic-Tock: A stunt that is held in a static position on one leg. Base(s) takes a downward dip and releases top person in an upward fashion, as the top person switches his or her weight to the other leg and lands in a static position on the opposite leg. The dip may or may not pass through prep level before release.

Toe/Leg Pitch: A single- or multi-based toss in which the base(s) push upward on a single foot or leg of the top person to increase the top person's height.

Toss: An airborne stunt where a base(s) executes throwing motion from waist level to increase height of top person. The top person becomes free from all bases, and is free from performing surface when toss is initiated (ex: basket toss or sponge toss). Note: Toss to hands, toss to extended stunts, and toss chair are *not* included in this category.

Top Person: See "Flyer."

Transitional Pyramid: A top person moving from one stunt to another. The transition may involve changing bases, however at least one person at prep level or below must maintain constant contact with the top person.

STANDING TUMBLING

STUNT

STRAIGHT RIDE

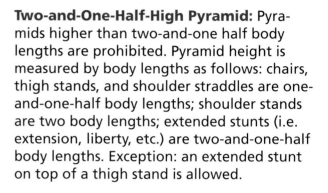

Transitional Stunt: Top person or top persons moving from one stunt to another thereby changing the configuration of the beginning stunt.

Traveling Toss: A toss which intentionally requires the bases or catchers to move in a certain direction to catch the top person. (This does not include a quarter turn by the bases in tosses such as kick full.)

Tuck Arch: Similar to kick arch, except instead of a kick it is an arch out of a tuck position.

Tuck Position: A position in which the knees and hips are bent and drawn into the chest; the body is bent at the waist.

Tumbling: Any gymnastic or acrobatic skill executed on the performing surface.

Twist: Rotation around the body's vertical axis while airborne.

Twisting Mount: Mounts that begin with a twisting motion of the top person within the vertical axis (can be as few as one-quarter twist up to two twisting rotations) that end up either a) in a prep-level stunt, b) in a loading position prior to the execution of a stunt, or c) in a fully extended stunt.

Twisting Toss: Any type of toss that involves the top person rotating at least one-quarter rotation around the vertical axis of the body.

Two-High Pyramid: All top persons must be primarily supported by a base(s) who is in direct weight-bearing contact with the performing surface.

Two-and-One-Half-High Pyramid: Pyramids higher than two-and-one half body lengths are prohibited. Pyramid height is measured by body lengths as follows: chairs, thigh stands, and shoulder straddles are one-and-one-half body lengths; shoulder stands are two body lengths; extended stunts (i.e. extension, liberty, etc.) are two-and-one-half body lengths. Exception: an extended stunt on top of a thigh stand is allowed.

Two-Leg Extended Stunt: Extended stunts that are above prep level in which the top person is bearing weight on both feet and both feet are in the hands of the base(s).

Walkover: A non-aerial acrobatic skill involving hip-over-head rotation in which a person rotates forward or backward (usually performed with the legs in a split position) with support from one or both hands.

Whip: Flip or somersault, with the feet coming up over the head and the body rotating around the axis of the waist, while the body remains in an arched position (not tucked and not in layout position). A whip has the look of a back handspring without the hands contacting the ground.

Wolf-Wall Transition: Transition that involves the main top person traveling over (front to back, back to front, or side to side) a bracing top person's leg (at prep level). The leg of the bracing top person is extended away from the body and connected (foot to waist) to a third top person at prep level.

X-Out: Flip or somersault skill performed that involves spreading the arms and legs into an "X" during the rotation of the flip.

TWIST

TUCK POSITION

X-OUT

RESOURCE GUIDE

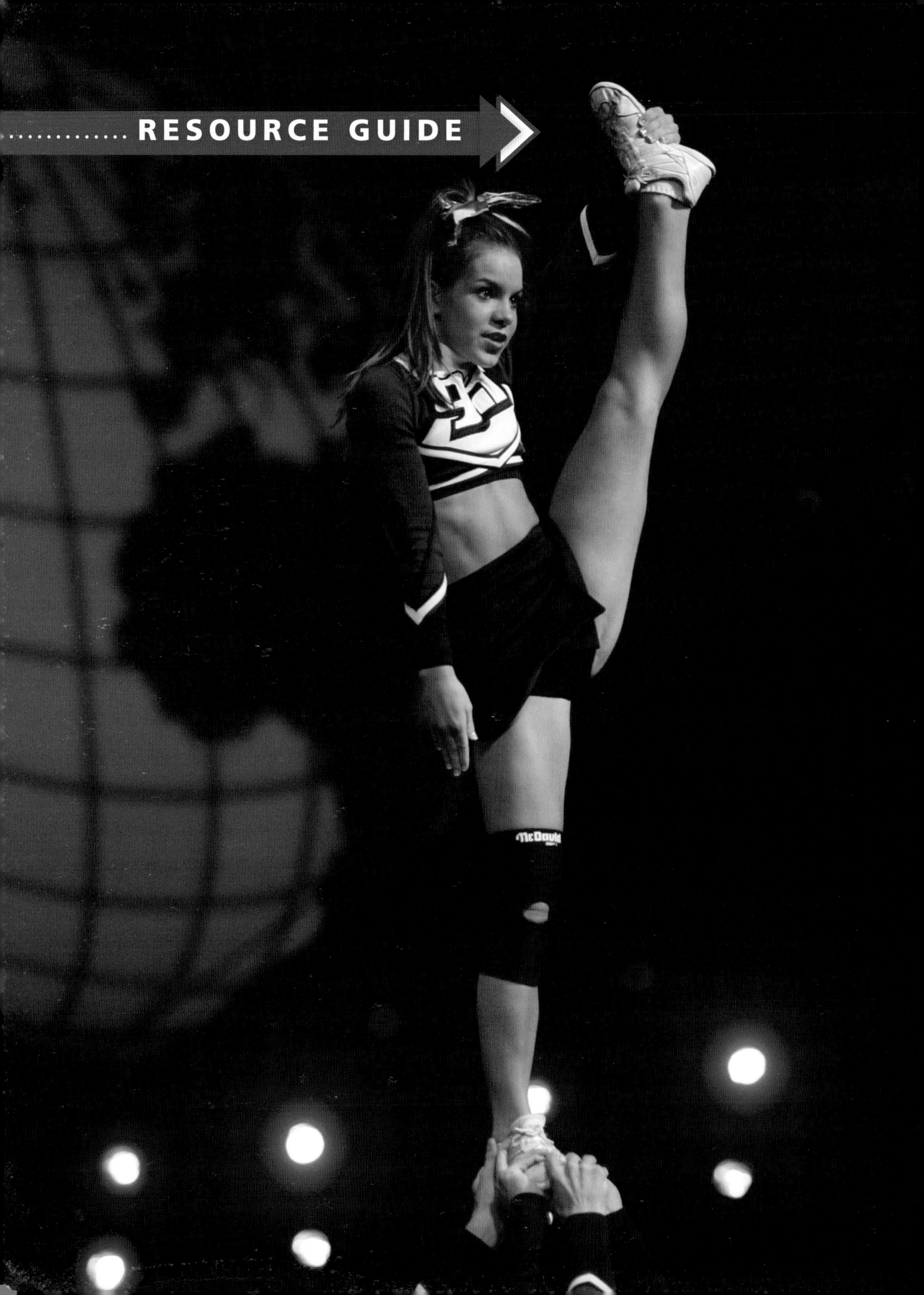

Cheer Organizations:

American Association of Cheerleading Coaches and Administrators (AACCA)
6745 Lenox Center Court, Ste 318
Memphis, TN 38115
800-533-6583
www.aacca.org

National All Star Cheerleading Coaches Congress (NACCC)
6745 Lenox Center Court, Ste 300
Memphis, TN 38115
800-829-6237
www.usasf.net

National Council for Spirit Safety and Education (NCSSE)
P.O. BOX 311192
Enterprise, AL 36331-1192
1-866-45-NCSSE
www.spiritsafety.com

Nation's Leading Cheer Companies (NLCC)
PO Box 707
Church Hill, TN 37642
877-256-6522
www.nlccfinaldestination.com

Spirit Industry Trade Association (SITA)
6992 Dublin Road
Dublin, OH 43017
800-477-8868
www.spiritindustrytrade.com

U.S. All Star Federation (USASF)
6745 Lenox Center Court, Ste 300
Memphis, TN 38115
800-829-6237
www.usasf.net

Cheer Competition Companies:

All-Star Challenge
4907 S. Alston Ave.
Durham, NC 27713
877-997-9599
www.allstarchallenge.com

The American Championships
PO Box 15267
Gainesville, FL 32604
800-462-8294 ext: 132
www.spiritteam.com

America's Best Championships
PO Box 2469
Addison, TX 75001
800-414-8778
www.americasbestcheer.com

American Cheerleaders Association
7415 Northaven Dr
Dallas, TX 75230
800-316-8815
www.acanationals.com

American Cheer Power
201 Spruce Dr
Dickinson, TX 77539
800-500-0840
www.cheerpower.com

AmeriCheer
20 Collegeview Rd
Westerville, OH 43081
800-966-JUMP
www.americheer.com

Athletic Championships
2847 John Deere Dr Ste 102
Knoxville, TN 37917
866-894-7848
www.athleticchampionships.com

Champion Cheer & Dance!
3200 Tanager St
Raleigh, NC 27606
800-732-2309
www.championcupnationals.com

Cheer Ltd., Inc.
118 Ridgeway Dr Ste 101
Fayetteville, NC 28311
800-477-8868
http://cheerltd.com

CHEERSPORT
11011 Monroe Rd Ste C
Matthews, NC 28105
888-READY-OK
www.cheersport.net

Cheer Tech
35 Fairmont Ave
Laurel Springs, NJ 08021
866-52-CHEER
www.cheertech.net

Christian Cheerleaders of America (CCA)
PO Box 49
Bethania, NC 27010
877-CHEERCA
www.cheercca.com

COA Cheer & Dance
3699 Paragon Dr
Columbus, OH 43228
877-490-0010
www.coacheeranddance.com

Coastal Alliance Corporation
825 Hammonds Ferry Rd Ste H-J
Linthicum, MD 21090
866-946-2232
www.thecoastalcorporation.com

Deep South Cheer and Dance, Inc.
PO Box 2462
Madison, MS 39130
601-605-1055
www.deepsouthcheer.com

JAMfest Cheer and Dance
11500 Champions Way
Louisville, KY 40299
866-JAMFEST
www.jamfest.com

Jamz Cheer & Dance
PO Box 4308
Modesto, CA 95352
800-920-4272
www.jamz.com

National Cheerleaders Association
2010 Merritt Dr
Garland, TX 75041
800-NCA-2-WIN
www.nationalspirit.com

Nations Best Championships
3918 Tumbleweed Ct
Lawrence, KS 66049
785-843-8711
www.nbchamps.com

Spirit Cheer
1809 E Broadway St Ste 339
Oviedo, FL 32765
888-716-2287
www.spiritcheer.com

Spirit Unlimited
777 Rte 3 N Ste G
Gambrills, MD 21054
888-737-2221
www.spiritunlimited.com

United Spirit Association
11135 Knott Ave, Suite C
Cypress, CA 90630
800-886-4USA
www.usacamps.com

Universal Cheerleaders Association (UCA)
6745 Lenox Center Court, Ste 300
Memphis, TN 38115
888-CHEER-UCA
www.varsity.com

USA Sports Production
PO Box 29185
Indianapolis, IN 46229
317-891-8260
www.championscupseries.com

US Spirit
PO Box 26701
Columbus, OH 43226
800-469-7878
www.us-spirit.com

United Performing Association, Inc. (UPA)
11101 Zealand Ave N
Champlin, MN 55316
800-800-6872
www.upainc.net

Universal Spirit
598 Indian Trail Road South #229
Indian Trail, NC 28079
704-821-4872
www.universalspiritassociation.com

World Cheerleading Association (WCA)
PO Box 220098
St. Louis, MO 63122
888-TEAM-WCA
www.cheerwca.com

World Spirit Federation
1062 S Batesville Rd
Greer, SC 29650
877-WSFCHEER
www.wsfcheer.com

Cheer Camp Companies:

American Cheer Power
201 Spruce
Dickinson, TX 77539
800-500-0840
www.cheerpower.com

American Cheerleaders Association
7415 Northaven
Dallas, TX 75230
800-316-8815
www.acacheerleading.com

Americheer
20 Collegeview Rd
Westerville, OH 43081
800-966-JUMP
www.americheer.com

Cheer Ltd.
118 Ridgeway Dr, Ste 101
Fayetteville, NC 28311
800-477-8868
www.cheerltd.com

Cheer Tech
35 Fairmont Ave
Laurel Springs, NJ 08021
866-52-CHEER
www.cheertech.net

Cheerleading Technique Camps (CTC)
PO Box 15267
Gainesville, FL 32604
800-462-8294 ext: 132
www.spiritteam.com

CHEERSPORT
11011 Monroe Rd, Ste C
Matthews, NC 28105
888-READY-OK
www.cheersport.net

Christian Cheerleaders of America (CCA)
PO Box 49
Bethania, NC 27010
877-CHEERCA
www.cheercca.com

COA Cheer & Dance
3699 Paragon Dr
Columbus, OH 43228
877-490-0010
www.coacheer.com

Coastal Camps – Coastal Alliance Corporation
825 Hammonds Ferry Rd Ste H-J
Linthicum, MD 21090
866-946-2232
www.thecoastalcorporation.com

Deep South Cheer and Dance, Inc.
PO Box 2462
Madison, MS 39130
601-605-1055
www.deepsouthcheer.com

JAMfest Cheer and Dance
11500 Champions Way
Louisville, KY 40299
866-JAMFEST
www.jamfest.com

Jamz Cheer & Dance
PO Box 4308
Modesto, CA 95352
800-920-4272
www.jamz.com

National Cheerleaders Association
2010 Merritt Dr
Garland, TX 75041
800-NCA-2-WIN
www.nationalspirit.com

One Up All Star Performance Camps
2847 John Deere Dr Ste 102
Knoxville, TN 37917
877-366-6387
www.do-oneup.com

Panama City Beach Cheer Camp, Inc.
PO Box 9595
Panama City Beach, FL 32417
866-243-7822
www.panamacitycheercamp.com

Super CDA
PO Box 957491
Hoffman Estates, IL 60195
847-975-5500
www.supercda.com

Universal Cheerleaders Association (UCA)
6745 Lenox Center Ct, Ste 300
Memphis, TN 38115
888-CHEER-UCA
www.varsity.com

Cheer Uniforms:

Cheerleader & DanzTeam (CDT)
6745 Lenox Center Court, Suite 300
Memphis, TN 38115
800-533-8022
www.nationalspirit.com

Cheerleading Company
11350 Hillguard Rd
Dallas, TX 75243
800-411-4105
www.cheerleading.com

Cran Barry, Inc
330C Lynnway
Lynn, MA 01903
800-992-2021
www.cranbarry.com

Deep South Cheer
PO Box 2462
Madison, MS 39130
866-DSC-2DAY
www.deepsouthcheer.com

Dehen Cheer & Dance
2701 SE 14th Avenue
Portland, OR 97202
800-547-0473
www.dehencheer.com

Spirit Innovations
PO Box 2469
Addison, TX 75001
800-414-8778
www.spiritinnovations.com

TeamLeader
2901 Summit Ave St 300
Plano, TX 75074
877-365-7555
www.teamleader.com

Varsity Spirit Fashions
6745 Lenox Center Ct Ste 300
Memphis, TN 38115
800-4VARSITY
www.varsity.com

 ## Cheer Shoes:

Adidas
5055 N Greeley Ave
Portland, OR 97217
800-448-1796
www.adidas.com

Asics America Corporation
16275 Laguna Canyon Rd
Irvine, CA 92618
800-678-9435
www.asicsamerica.com

Converse
One High Street
North Andover, MA 01845
800-554-2667
www.converse.com

Kaepa USA, Inc.
9050 Autobahn Dr, Ste 500
Dallas, TX 75237
800-880-9200
www.kaepa.com

New Balance
Brighton Landing, 20 Guest St
Boston, MA 02135
800-253-7463
www.newbalance.com

Nfinity Products, Inc.
1401 Peachtree St #500
Atlanta, GA 30309
404-870-3558
www.nfinityshoes.com

Nike
PO Box 4027
Beaverton, OR 97076
800-344-6453
www.nike.com

Power Cheer
Power USA
37 Mountian Blvd. #5
Warren, NJ 07059
800-437-2526
www.power-cheer.com

Reebok
1895 J. W. Foster Blvd.
Canton, MA 02021
781-401-5000
www.reebok.com

Zephz
110 Industrial Dr. Ste 101
Pottstown, PA 19464
610-495-8070
www.zephz.com

ACKNOWLEDGEMENTS ···········

Developing this book has been, without a doubt, a team effort, and we would like to extend a heartfelt thanks to several people who played an integral role in this process. First, to our publisher Charles Miers, our editor Caitlin Leffel, our copy editor Susan Homer and our proofreader Tricia Levi. You all have been absolutely terrific throughout the project, and we appreciate your dedication and support. We owe a debt of gratitude to our representation at Shade Global and our good friend Sheryl Shade, who brought this opportunity to us and supported us all along the way. A special thanks goes to Jim Chadwick, Steve Peterson, and the entire staff of the U.S. All Star Federation (USASF) for working with us to include the USASF glossary of terms and outstanding photography from the Cheer Worlds. We would also like to thank Lawrence "Herkie" Herkimer, Jeff Webb, Sara McDaniel, Ryan Martin, David Hanbery, Brooklyn Freitag, Cassondra Machac, and Blanche Kapustin for sharing, in their own words, their experiences in cheerleading through the "My Story" segments, which added valuable perspective to the book. We'd also like to extend a word of appreciation to all of the competition and camp organizations who provided photographs from their events, which so vibrantly illustrated the depth of cheerleading today. And finally, to Mark Pettit and our office mates at the marketing firm Creaxion, thank you for putting up with us, especially as each deadline loomed!

PHOTO CREDITS

The American Championships/Universal Event Photography
p. 30 (row two/photo one)

America's Best Championships/ Action Pitstop Photography
p. 30 (row one/photo one), p. 75 (top)

AmeriCheer
p. 16 (bottom), p. 22 (bottom right), p. 30 (row three/photo one), p. 64 (right), p. 113

Cassondra Machac
p. 107 (left)

Charles Kent
p. 22 (left), p. 46 (3), p. 56 (2), p. 95 (middle)

Chuck Perry Photography
p. 1, p. 14 (bottom), p. 23 (both), p. 24, p. 25, p. 49, p. 50 (bottom), p. 57 (left), p. 58, p. 59 (left), p. 116

Cheer Ltd./Universal Event Photography
p. 3, p. 31 (row three/photo five), p. 52, p. 65, p. 66, p. 135 (bottom right)

CHEERSPORT
p. 5 (second), p. 22 (top right), p. 28, p. 31 (row two/photo three), p. 77

Cheerleaders of America (COA)/Tim Jackson
p. 31 (row one/photo two), p. 76 (bottom), p. 80, p. 98

Donnell Field/Field Imagery
p. 5 (eighth), p. 39, p. 57 (right), p. 109, p. 110

Karim Shamsi-Basha
p. 47, p. 92, p. 95 (bottom)

Kenny Wisniewski
p. 16 (top right), p. 17

Lightspeed Photos/Jamfest Events
p. 31 (row three/photo four), p. 72

Elizabeth G. Rosetti
p. 16 (bottom)

National Cheerleaders Association
p. 5 (top), p. 9, p. 10, p. 13 (both), p. 19 (both), p. 87

Panama City Beach Cheer Camps
p. 68

Phillip Dupree Photography
p. 59 (left)

Reed B Hogan MD
p. 15 (bottom), p. 26, p. 27,

JAMZ Cheer and Dance/RT Productions
p. 31 (row one/photo three)

Donna Martin
p. 69

Scott Einuis
p. 5 (fourth), p. 11, p. 18 (left), p. 30 (2/leftmost), p. 50 (top), p. 53, p. 54, p. 55 (2), p. 61, p. 62, p. 67, p. 71, p. 76 (top), p. 82, p. 86 (right), p. 95 (top), p. 97, p. 99, p. 100, p. 101, p. 104 -105 (8), p. 106 (6), p. 107 (2), p. 125 (3), p. 127 (top), p. 129 (3 right), p. 131 (bottom 2), p. 133 (bottom right), p. 135 (top, bottom left), p. 137 (3)

Shane Paulson
p. 34, p. 35, p. 78

Spirit Cheer
p. 31 (row two/photo two), p. 74 (top)

Spirit Innovations
p. 90, p. 91, p. 141

Steven Michael Studios
p. 5 (sixth), p. 85, p. 94

TeamLeader
p. 90 (right), p. 143

Threads-of-Fun
p. 64 (left)

Tim Jackson
p. 14 (top), p. 15 (top), p. 21, p. 32, p. 43, p. 44, p. 48 (2), p. 112, p. 114, p. 115, p. 118, p. 119, p. 120, p. 127, p. 129 (left)

UCA/Universal Event Photography
p. 31 (row three/photo three), p. 73 (2), p. 74 (bottom), p. 75 (bottom), p. 131 (top right), p. 133

USASF/Universal Event Photography
p. 5 (third, fourth, sixth), p. 16 (top), p. 18 (right), p. 30 (row three/ photo two), p. 41, p. 83, p. 100 (top left), p. 103 (2), p. 123-124, p. 131 (top)

Varsity Brands
p. 4, p. 11 (first, second), p. 37 (3), p. 42, p. 63

Varsity Spirit Fashions
p. 86 (left), p. 88-89 (24), p. 93, p. 139